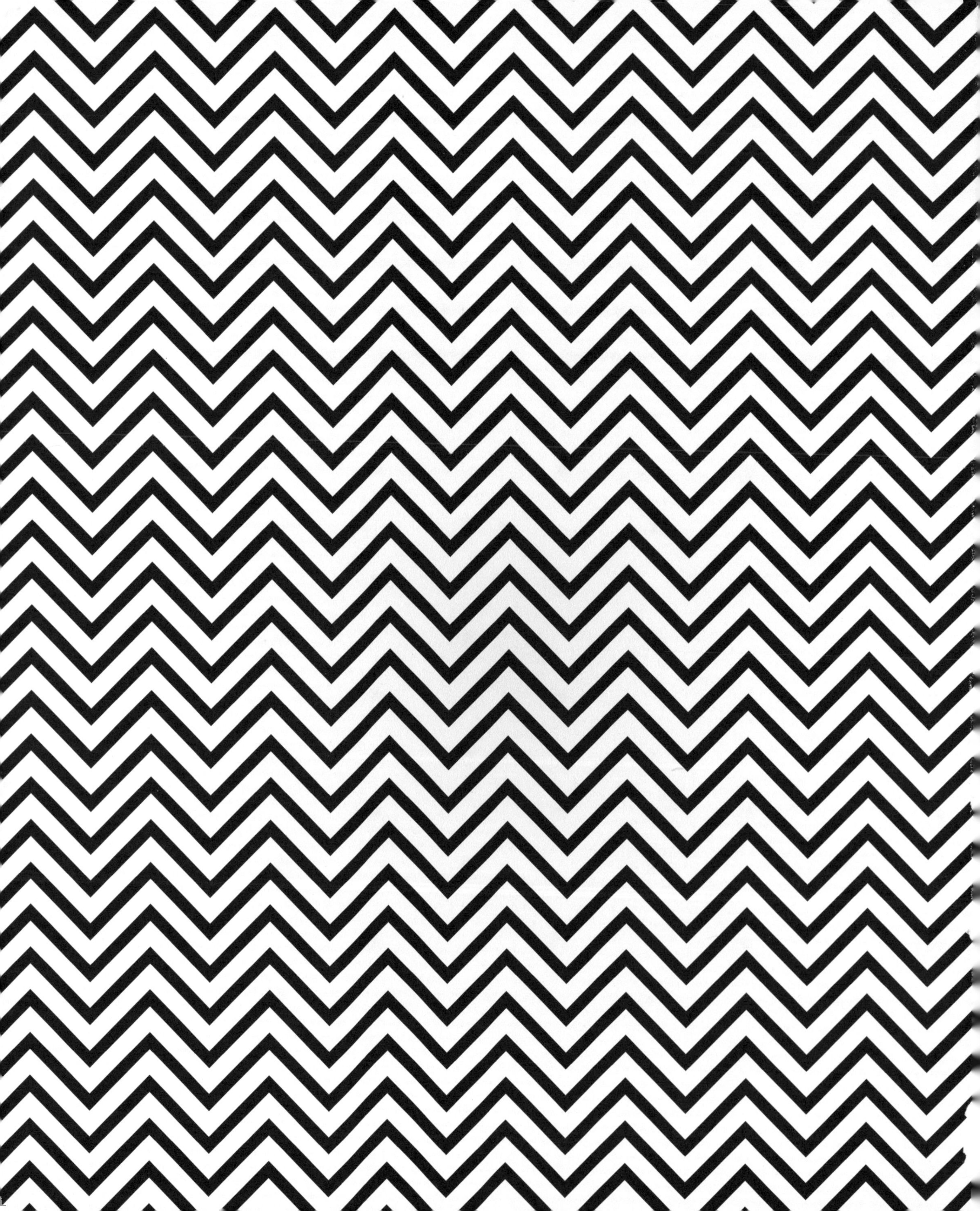

JAMEA RICHMOND-EDWARDS

ANCIENT FUTURE

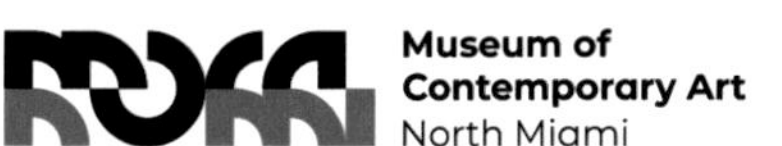

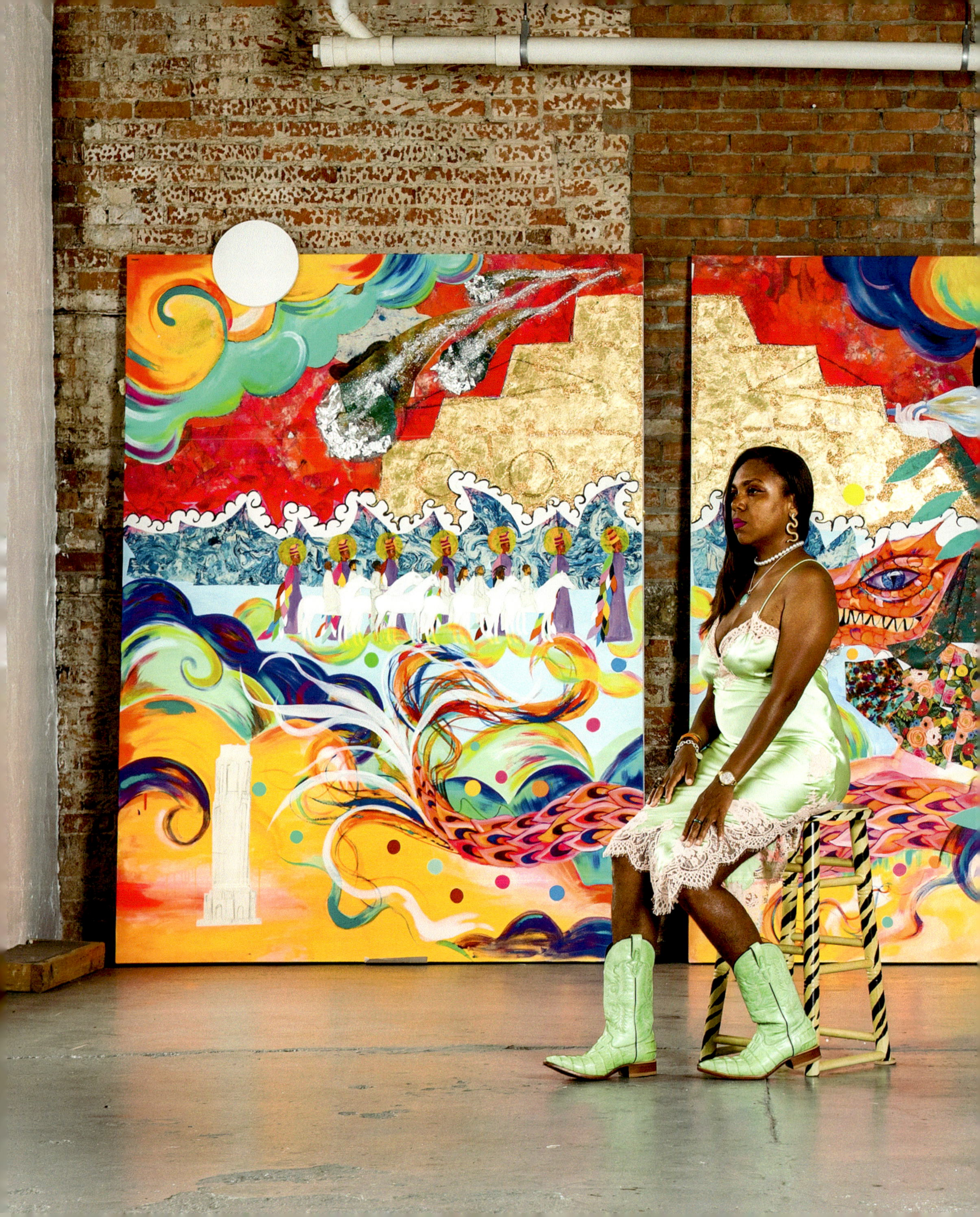

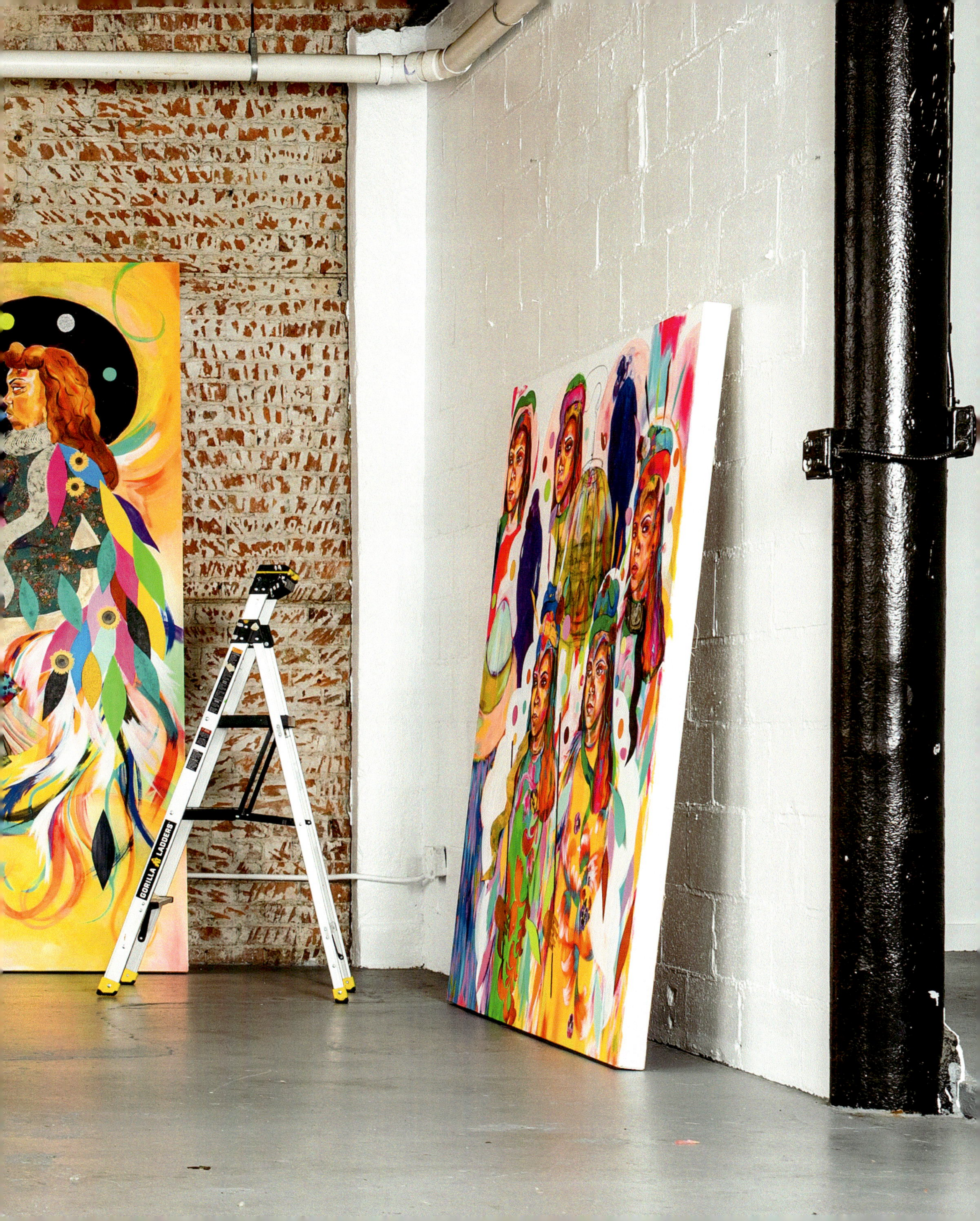
GORILLA LADDERS

CONTENTS

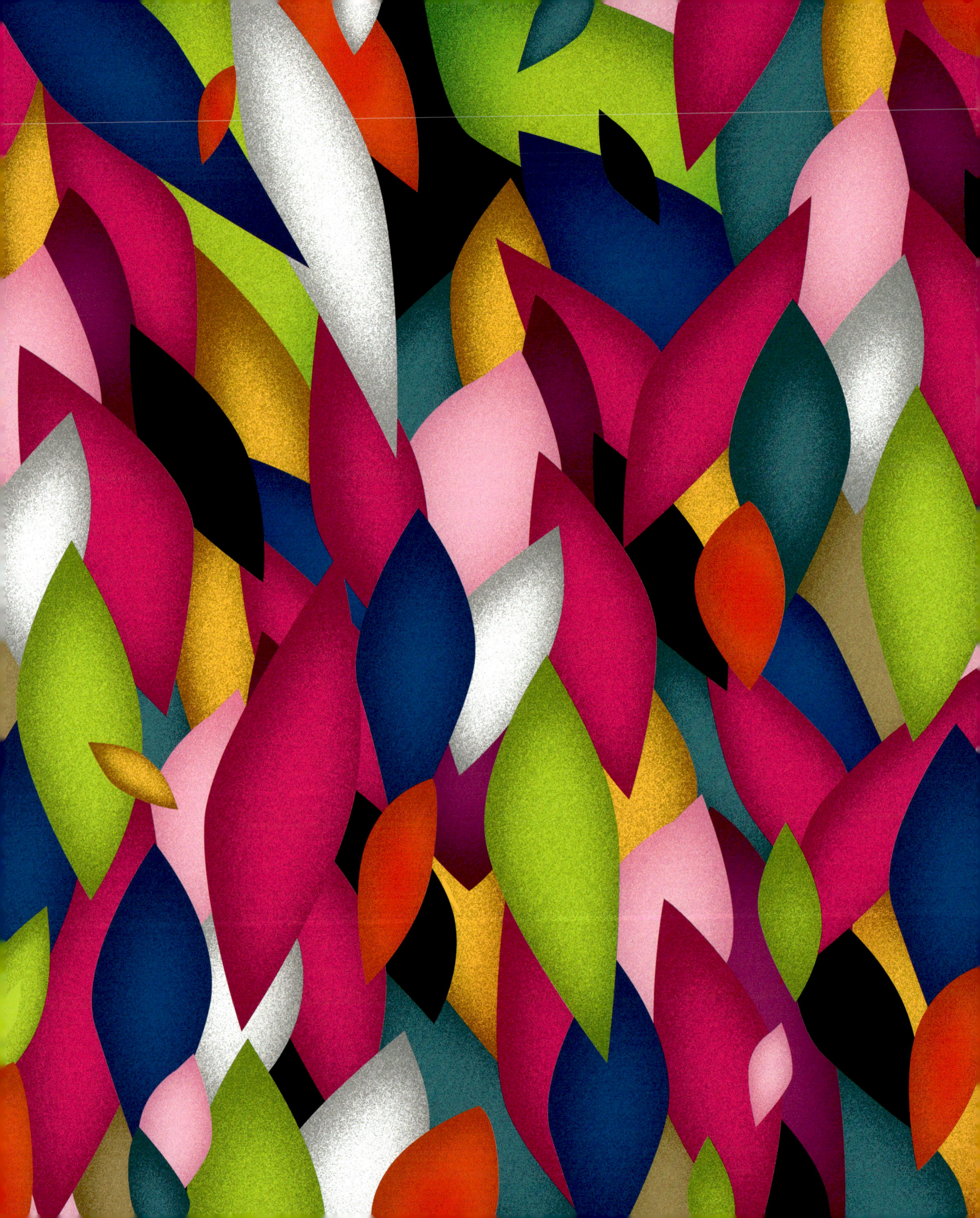

FOREWORD

CHANA BUDGAZAD SHELDON

As I complete my sixth year leading the Museum of Contemporary Art, North Miami (MOCA), and as the museum approaches its thirtieth anniversary, I am proud to affirm that championing artists at critical moments in their careers remains a vital component of our mission. In 2018, MOCA presented *AfriCOBRA: Messages to the People*, a pivotal exhibition for the institution, which featured several artists who were mentors to Jamea Richmond-Edwards. It was an honor to provide a platform for AfriCOBRA artists to celebrate the fiftieth anniversary of their collective, just as it is an honor to support a new generation of younger or emerging artists. When I first saw Jamea Richmond-Edwards's work at the Prizm Art Fair several years ago, I knew she was an artist on the brink of something special.

With *Ancient Future*, Richmond-Edwards boldly intervenes in the flexible architecture of our gallery walls and deposits a pyramid in the center of our exhibition space. This symbolic gesture acts as a physical representation of creation and divine renewal, while also gesturing toward the purposeful excavation of history. It encourages visitors and the museum itself to think about how we create new ideas from old, and the ways in which the symbolism of the ancients can help guide the strides we take toward a future we can't see. The paintings of *Ancient Future*, alongside a newly commissioned film, invite us to expand our minds toward a new kind of thinking that refuses to leave the past behind, even as it imagines a new, more inclusive future.

More than just an art museum, MOCA is a space for supporting conversations, taking risks, and encouraging the development of artists' voices. While our mission has evolved over the past three decades—and continues to do so—our commitment to connecting diverse communities and cultures by creating access to groundbreaking contemporary art has been constant throughout. *Jamea Richmond-Edwards: Ancient Future* also commemorates the first authored show by our first full-time curator in over a decade, Adeze Wilford, who I am fortunate and grateful to have as my colleague. My heartfelt appreciation extends to the entire MOCA team, all of whom worked together to help realize Jamea Richmond-Edwards's vision.

This exhibition is made possible by the generosity of our key funders. Thank you to the Andy Warhol Foundation for the Visual Arts and Kravets Wehby Gallery. MOCA North Miami is generously funded by the John S. and James L. Knight Foundation and the Miami-Dade County Department of Cultural Affairs and the Cultural Affairs Council, the Miami-Dade County Mayor and Board of County Commissioners. Founding support for the MOCA Sustainability Fund was provided by the Green Family Foundation Trust.

My deepest thanks and appreciation to MOCA's dedicated board of trustees. Led by its chairman, William M. Lehman, Jr., the board's support has been and continues to be critical to the success of our institution. I sincerely thank the City of North Miami Mayor and Council and the North Miami City Manager, Rasha Cameau, MBA, FRA-RP, for their continued partnership and support.

Finally, thank you, Jamea. I am grateful for your trust and your thoughtful collaboration with MOCA. We are thrilled to host your largest solo presentation of new commissions in a museum space.

Chana Budgazad Sheldon
Executive Director, Museum of Contemporary Art, North Miami

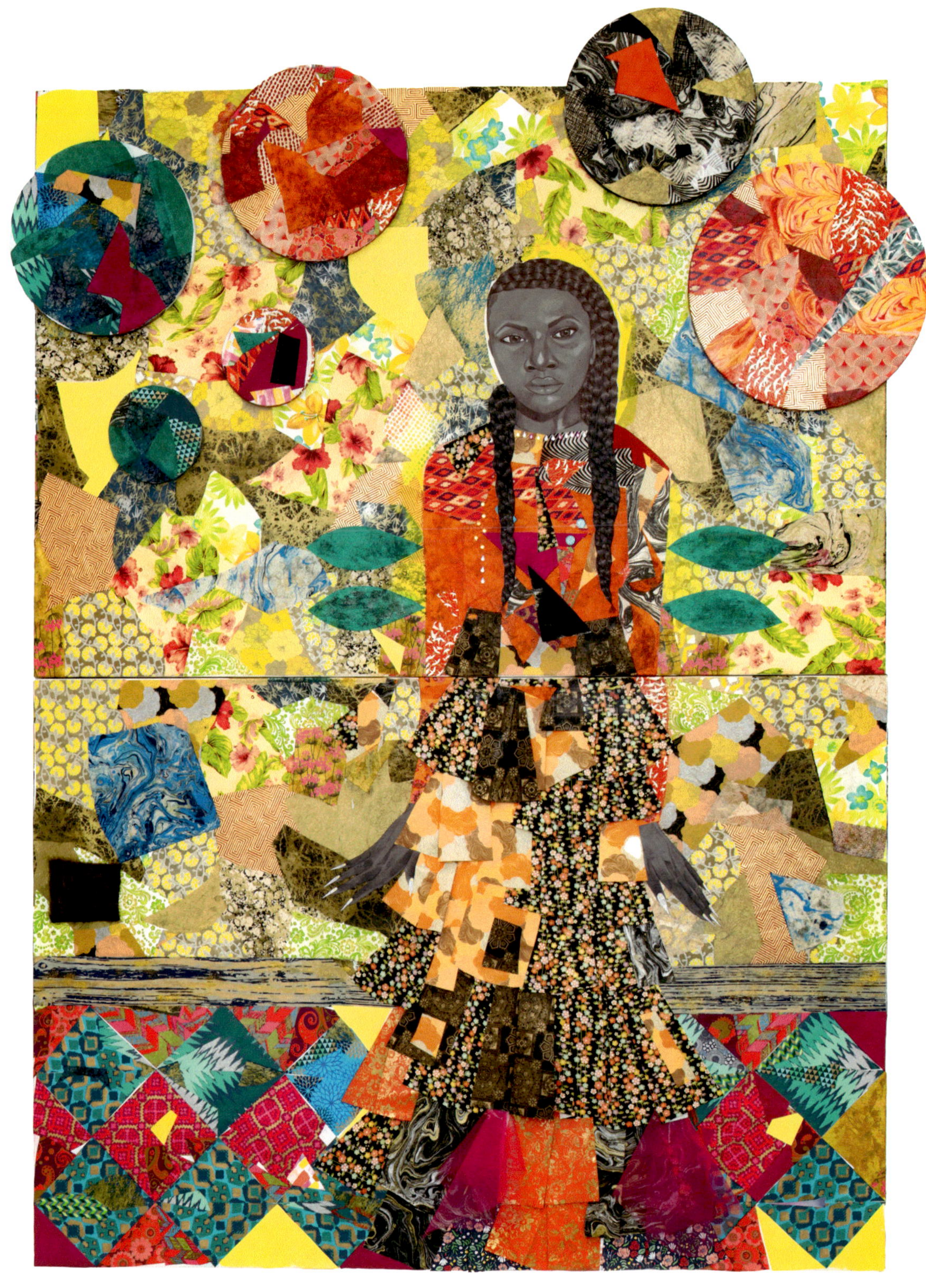

The Prettiest Dress (diptych), 2019
Ink, acrylic, mixed media, colored pencil, fabric, glitter, and rhinestones on canvas
96 × 72 in. overall

IMAGINING A WORLD OF HER/OUR OWN

ADEZE WILFORD

In the Afrofuturist imaginary, it is as imperative to transform the ordinary into the extraordinary as it is to consider the everyday within the impossible. —Zoe Whitley

A world apart
A world within
Ancient and luminous
The before before and the hereafter
—Saul Williams

In popular culture narratives, when the future is considered, it is often in one of two ways: as a gleaming technologically advanced super metropolis or a dystopian ghost town devoid of the strides made in decades past. This binary of lack and plenty speaks to a particular limitation of imagination that is found in the West. For artist Jamea Richmond-Edwards, the future is full; it doesn't fall into the tropes of shimmering city or dusty wasteland. Instead, in her imagination, the future is a blend of old and new becoming something as yet undreamed. It builds on what we already know and hold familiar, but the world the artist is creating seeks to be fully removed from the rigid binaries of race and gender that stifle our collective reality. *Ancient Future* is the largest solo museum presentation of Richmond-Edwards's work to date and is ambitious in both scale and media. Creating narratives across canvas, intricate collages and drawings on paper, and large-scale film installation, the collective body of work uses influences from the artist's experience at Jackson State University, her childhood in and subsequent return to Detroit, and references to current events. While her earlier work featured Black figures rendered in tones of gray, a shift in her practice brought both natural skin tones and more clearly recognizable self-portraits. Collectively, *Ancient Future* represents an artist who is unearthing a new aspect of her practice both in the physical presentation of her work as well as its content. Engaging with the cosmos, self-fashioning, and new mythologies, this exhibition is the work of an artist creating her own way through building a new world.

Major influences on the artist's subject matter are the three cities she has called home. Critically, each of them has had a large Black population that has had strong middle-class and academic opportunities, and each of them has also gone through economic blight and been impacted by gentrification and the pushing out of the very communities that comprised their vibrant fabric. A recent article in the *Detroit Free Press* discusses the constricting of the city's Black residents according to the census, asserting that, "Detroit stands out nationally for share of its Black population. Some big cities in the US have more Black residents than Detroit such as Chicago or New York. But in those two cities, Black residents make up a smaller share of their total population compared to Detroit. On this measure—the share of Black residents in a city—Detroit, with Black residents

Epigraphs: Zoe Whitley, "The Place Is Space: Afrofuturism's Transnational Geographies," in *The Shadows Took Shape*, ed. Naima J. Keith and Zoe Whitley (New York: Studio Museum in Harlem, 2013), 22; "Pedagogue of Young Gods," track 16 on Saul Williams, *The Inevitable Rise and Liberation of Niggy Tardust!*, Fader Label FL-0906, 2008, compact disc.

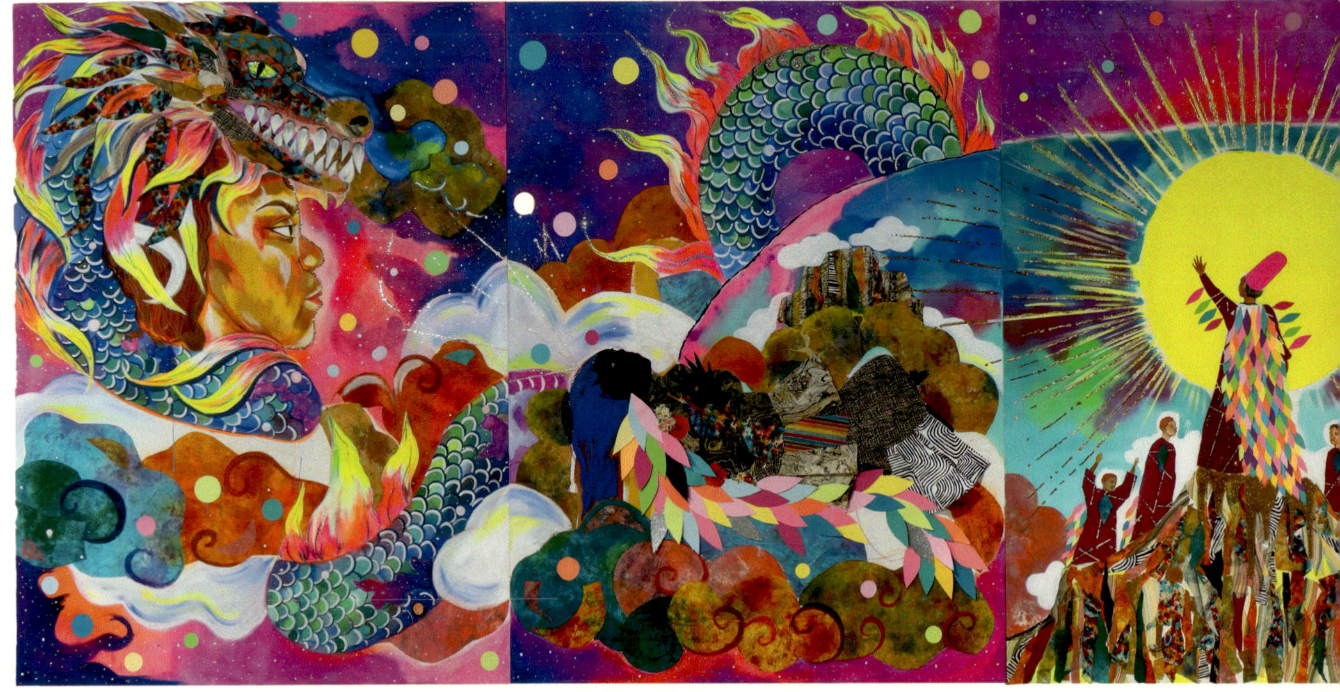

accounting for more than three-quarters of the city's population, looks more like Jackson, Mississippi."[1] Detroit having this concentration of Blackness undoubtedly influenced the artist. The importance of Black business owners, including the artist's own family members—automotive workers and creatives, including musicians—created a culture that is unique to the city and is both traditionally glamorous and experimental, and which is present in the artist's work. The foundational experience of attending Jackson State University in Mississippi is also a large part of the work in the exhibition, most obviously seen in the film installation from which the show takes its name. *Ancient Future* is a homage to the artist's experience in the HBCU's legendary marching band. Just before the pandemic, the artist moved from the Washington, DC, metro area back to her hometown of Detroit. Her life spent moving between these three Black meccas is vital to understanding her work. There is no way to dream of an alternative future if one isn't already exposed to the impact of a majority-Black space. Artist and activist Alisha Wormsley coined the simple phrase "There Are Black People in the Future" that was installed on a billboard in Pennsylvania in 2018. Originally tongue in cheek, it became a larger part of the more recent Afrofuturist movement, especially when the work was controversially removed from the installation after community intervention.[2] Meant to disrupt the tropes of popular media engaging with the futuristic, such as *The Jetsons* or *Dune*, this statement calls attention to the absence of Black people in depictions of the future. For Richmond-Edwards, coming of age in and thriving in these predominately Black spaces, there was no question that the future would be populated by Black people—in fact, in the world she imagines, Blackness becomes an imperative.

While making this exhibition, during numerous conversations with the artist, the notion of her work existing in a space that is outside of the status quo and part of a punk or DIY zeitgeist became an additional lens through

1 Clara Hendrickson, Kristi Tanner, and Dana Afana, "Detroit's 40-Year Reign as Nation's Largest Majority-Black City May Be Over," *Detroit Free Press*, May 23, 2023, https://www.freep.com/story/news/local/2023/05/23/detroit-largest-black-city-census-population-duggan/70235685007/.

2 Sarah Rose Sharp, "Artist's Billboard Declaring 'There Are Black People in the Future' Taken Down by Landlord," *Hyperallergic*, April 9, 2018, https://hyperallergic.com/436763/alisha-wormsley-the-last-billboard-pittsburgh-there-are-black-people-in-the-future/.

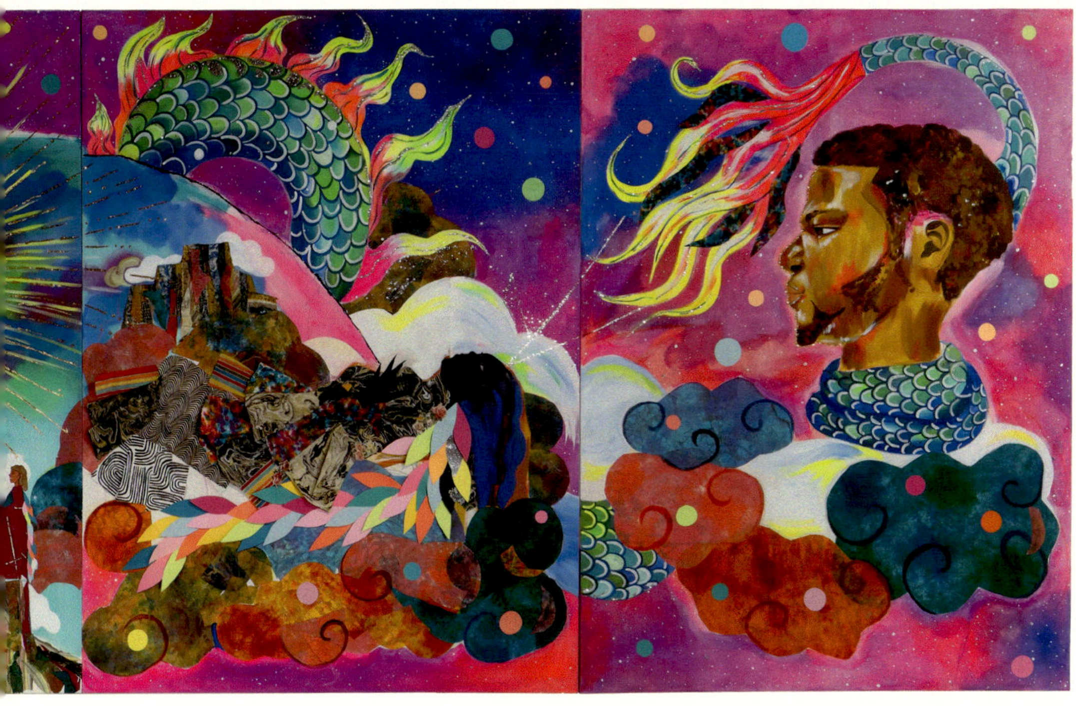

Dark Night of the Soul, 2023
Acrylic, gold leaf, glitter, mixed-media collage, and soft sculpture on canvas
96 × 360 in. overall

which to engage with the work. Richmond-Edwards creates in a space that is removed from dominant or expected expressions of Black representation and instead remixes canvases and patchworks collages in a visual language that is all her own. To quote DeForrest Brown, Jr., "Detroit techno, a concept of sonic world-building and coded information exchange borne out of a centuries-long lineage of African American struggle and insurrection, would eventually be exported, repackaged, and financialized within foreign markets . . . replicating the profit-oriented process of extraction."[3] Richmond-Edwards's work instead posits what happens when we don't give in to the extractive, what alchemy occurs when we redefine and reimagine a future that is ours, one that is deeply rooted within the histories and lineages of the past that were directly impacted by the transatlantic slave trade and the Great Migration, but also one that is rooted in a yearning for a future that leaves the particular trauma related to colonial greed and Western capitalism behind—a new frontier that calls upon the cosmos or investigates the depths of the ocean. This work forces us to interrogate how we make space for Black creativity that goes beyond the typical examples of production, consumption, and making. This is what the future looks like—expansion into space, not only planetary but also physical. What does utopia look like for an artist like Richmond-Edwards? Perfection is not the end goal; she instead creates a framework that doesn't leave it all behind but leaves just enough to create a new and powerful way of being, of seeing, of making.

Discussing the problem of the American racial binary system that is predicated on historical and present-day white supremacy, historian Isabel Wilkerson asserts, "Caste is more than rank, it is a state of mind that holds everyone captive, the dominant imprisoned in an illusion of their own entitlement, the subordinate trapped in the purgatory of someone else's definition of who they are and who they should be."[4] For Richmond-Edwards, this struggle for validation within one's own reality became

3 DeForrest Brown, Jr., *Assembling a Black Counter Culture* (New York: Primary Information, 2022), 16.

4 Isabel Wilkerson, *Caste: The Origins of Our Discontents* (New York: Random House, 2020), 290.

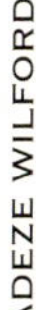

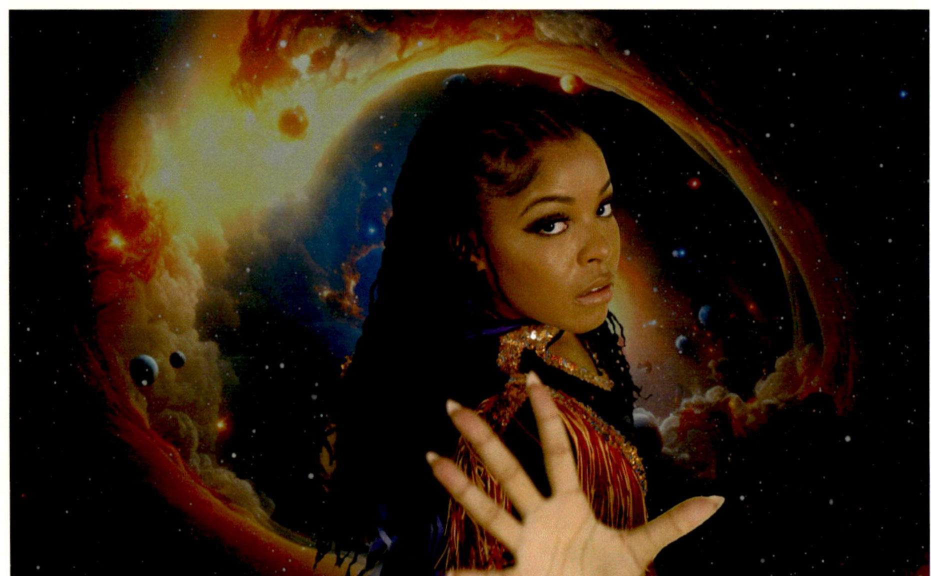

Ancient Future, 2023
Digital film, color, sound;
7 minutes

the impetus for making the works in this show. Her desire to envision a world without this stymied personhood was driven by a hopeful belief in the possibility of more beyond our current cultural dynamic. The caste system that is part of a larger global narrative but is especially felt within the context of the United States hurts equally the oppressed and the oppressor. It is mostly led by fear, the fear of a loss of power and the fear of a threat to oneself because of a lack of power. In this way, fear acts as a guiding principle for Black subjugation. For Richmond-Edwards, this body of work acts as divination that comes with its own particular kind of fear, the fear of being different. With the monumental painting *Dark Night of the Soul* she builds a new cosmos, one that flips the heavens and depths of the ocean, a new story of creationism that melds Egyptology with the biblical and adapts Detroit techno's own modern myth, Drexciya, which reimagines the birth of a civilization through the trauma of the transatlantic slave trade. Water, for the artist, is a source of both the unknown and chaos.[5] It has the transformative power to turn the body into something new and occupies a space either terrifying or fascinating. Bracketing a representation of the firmament are two figures of the goddess Nut, who was seen as "the regulator of the passage of days and nights, the movement of the sun and stars, therefore of time."[6] This level of power calls for outsize representation, a taking up of space. Spanning thirty feet, this monumental multi-canvas work renders goddess as giant, unapologetically. At its center, figures arise from the sea into a new pathway of discovery. Instead of space as the only place, the underexplored underwater becomes a world of possibility in equal measure. Across the canvas is a push and pull between above and below with the unknown future caught somewhere in between. Tapping into her own limitless creative expression, the artist leaned into this fear, this radical Black imagination, to forge the basis of this show to be unafraid to live in one's purpose, even if that means building a whole new world to see.

The multichannel video installation from which the exhibition takes its title, *Ancient Future*, is shown in an enclosed room in the shape of a pyramid. A reference to Egyptian and Mayan monuments, the artist uses a blend of historical reference points to build her mythos. In conversation with Tina Campt on his seminal video work *Love is the Message, The Message is Death,* Arthur Jafa posits that the power of Black music is the Black voice itself, stating, "We're the illegitimate prodigy of the West and we came to the Americas with this deep reservoir of culture and expressivity."[7] This particular kind of expressivity acts as an influential source for Rich-

5 Jamea Richmond-Edwards, conversation with author, July 11, 2023.

6 Susan Tower Hollis, "Women of Ancient Egypt and the Sky Goddess Nut," *The Journal of American Folklore* 100, no. 398 (October–December 1987): 499.

7 "*Love is the Message, The Message is Death:* Arthur Jafa in Conversation with Tina Campt," in *Black Futures*, ed. Kimberly Drew and Jenna Wortham (New York: One World, 2021), 65.

mond-Edwards's visual art practice. Often imitated but never quite fully replicated, the power of Black music across time from her beloved Detroit's industry-shifting Motown sound to Sun Ra's experimental jazz Arkestra to Saul Williams's poetic rap are integral touchstones within her practice. Played in her studio, these auditory expressions are part of the Black cultural experience and act as storytelling, sites of speculative history, and platforms for particular representations of Blackness. All these energies are present in the film, which uses appropriated speech from Sun Ra's iconic film *Space Is the Place* (1972) and features a score composed by the artist's son Jeremiah Edwards. Conceptually, *Ancient Future* is about the artist's own myth of goddesses reawakening after centuries. No longer bound by the planet, they move through space, in synchronized lock-step, building power from one another. Represented by a team of majorettes, a tradition and movement form that is influenced by the artist's time in Jackson State University's marching band, the famous Sonic Boom of the South, these goddesses are shown gliding through galaxies and their costumes reference the motif of elaborate cut feathers that runs throughout the exhibition. For the artist, showcasing intentional beauty and the history of this style of dancing is paramount. In a conversation in her studio prior to filming the dancers, the artist ruminated on the components of the installation and the content of the work, saying, "It speaks to that crown being the antenna to something even larger, the body being the antenna to something. Even the body is a temple. How we fashion our bodies, it falls along the lines of when you look in terms of the Mayan temples, when you look at the Egyptian temples, when you look in every corner of the planet and these markers of these mythological people who don't fucking exist anymore, you kind of see it. To me, I see the thread, I do. I don't know about everybody else. I also see the marker or those footprints in terms of that mythos with dance and movement."[8] This thread-pulling is embodied in the work, seen in the push and pull between the representation of powerful giant goddesses who are also young girls on the cusp of womanhood. The power of these portraits lies in the self-possession and embodiment of confidence these dancers are just beginning to tap into, existing in reality but also in the fictive cosmos Richmond-Edwards has conjured, in which a young girl has the power of a goddess and her beauty and lines give her the power to break and make worlds.

Throughout the making of the work for this exhibition and over the course of many conversations with the artist, the work of the vital speculative fiction author Octavia E. Butler became a touchstone. When asked why her focus was on writing stories that centered Black women, Butler stated, "When I began reading, I wasn't in any of this stuff I read . . . I wrote myself in, since I'm me and I'm here and I'm writing. I can write my own stories and I can write myself in."[9] This action of writing oneself into a narrative is not a phenomenon that is solely Butler's but is a frequent job of Black women, to constantly make space for ourselves and to do the work to ensure our stories, fictive or real, are not left out of the canon. Jamea Richmond-Edwards has used *Ancient Future* to push her practice, to develop a mythos that not only imagines Black people, Black women, in the future, but pictures them as luminous, larger than stars, world shakers and world makers.

8 Richmond-Edwards, conversation with author.

9 Octavia E. Butler, quoted in "We Tend to Do the Right Thing When We Get Scared," *New York Times*, January 1, 2000, https://www.nytimes.com/2000/01/01/books/visions-identity-we-tend-to-do-the-right-thing-when-we-get-scared.html.

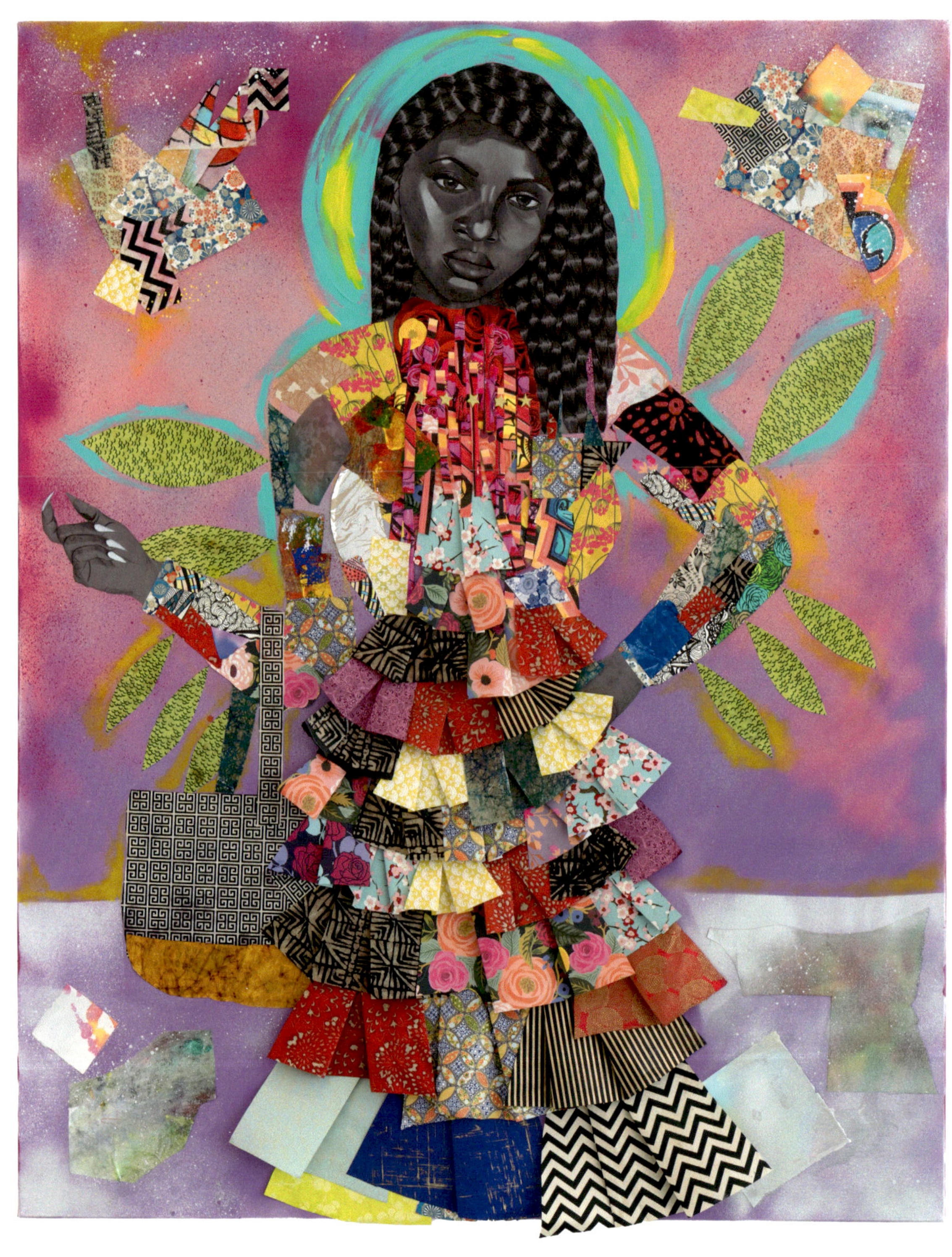

ARCHETYPE OF A 5 STAR, 2018
Acrylic, spray paint, glitter, ink, and
cut paper collage on canvas
60 × 48 in.

MYTHMAKING FOR THE PRESENT

TAYLOR RENEE ALDRIDGE

When I insert a figure into a painting space, I have to consider all of the things that it means and construct, edit and revise in order to reach its maximum effect so that [B]lackness becomes a noun, not an adjective. —Kerry James Marshall

In November 1988, the song "Good Life" by Detroit-based Techno music pioneer Kevin Saunderson was released. Under the moniker Inner City, the single disc carried the words INNER CITY GOOD LIFE in bold typeface. Voted one of the best dance songs of all time by *Rolling Stone*, "Good Life," an effort conceptualized, produced, and packaged out of 1980s Detroit, was released through immense irony. During the 1980s, Detroit was viewed by outsiders as a place filled with trauma, violence, blight, and Black failure from the 1960s to the present.[1] Despite its robust history of industrial innovation, in the later decades of the twentieth century, Detroit became a pejorative example for what *could* happen to an American city primarily occupied and led by African Americans. And, as John Leary has written, Detroit's post-1970 narrative was often reported through "spectacles of degradation."[2] Kevin Saunderson and Inner City's "Good Life" occupies a whole new meaning considering this context. The song functions as a balm in response to material decline that transpired in 1980s and '90s Detroit. And the song offers what could be viewed as a *sonic subversion*, broadcasting out to cities worldwide, to redress the flattened notions of what the City of Detroit is like.

The multidisciplinary artist Jamea Richmond-Edwards was raised in the foreground of this soundtrack and among such declines within the City of Detroit. Born in 1982, the artist's upbringing reflected the sociopolitical currents of that period, such as Reaganomics, industrial divestment, and the crack and HIV/AIDS epidemics. And as a child growing up in 1980s Detroit, she was surrounded by a range of effects from these broader macro currents, from familial loss to terse and precarious environments. However, this precarity and grief was not central to the ways in which Richmond-Edwards and other Black Detroiters defined their experiences during this era. Paradoxically, Detroit, even within its decline, offered a utopic space of rhizomatic Black creation and autonomy. A site that was purely self-referential, and unconcerned with white acceptability; naming for ourselves what should be valued. *The good life, our good life*.

Epigraph: Kerry James Marshall, quoted in Greg Tate, Charles Gaines, and Laurence Rassel, *Kerry James Marshall* (London: Phaidon, 2017), 29.

1 In the aftermath of the 1967 riots—Black civilians' response to decades of police brutality—many parcels in Detroit remained derelict for years, which instigated rapid white flight from the city into suburbs and a declining tax base. Known as a one-industry town, with great economic opportunity for much of the early twentieth century—a destination of many Black Alabamans and Georgians fleeing Jim Crow racial terror during the Great Migration—major auto companies began divesting from the city in the 1960s, leaving very little financial infrastructure for the primarily Black city residents. From 1971 to 1973, abuse of power by Detroit police tactical units under the STRESS initiative, in response to poverty and subsequent crime, caused an incredible amount of strain on Black American families through misplaced and erroneous convictions. In 1974, the city elected its first Black mayor, Coleman A. Young, a vibrant and vocal figure, who was championed by Black Detroiters, and criticized by white suburbanites as an emblem for everything that had gone wrong in the city.

2 John Patrick Leary, "Detroitism," *Guernica*, January 15, 2011, https://www.guernicamag.com/leary_1_15_11/.

The material culture of this specific epoch in Detroit history is filled with vernacular signifiers. This culture rendered a visual culture of success that decentered the white gaze and championed African American experience. The city and Richmond-Edwards's work, which celebrates it, cause us to question, *What kind of aesthetics and sonics are championed in a space that celebrates and prioritizes Black subjectivity over whiteness? How are both familial and civic inheritance carried out in a space like Detroit, which has such a unique Indigenous history, one of the last stops on the Underground Railroad before enslaved Africans found freedom in other countries,*[3] *and a former "sanctuary city" for undocumented Americans?*[4] Detroit's modern narrative is often flattened because its history centers those who are often marginalized and thus not the narrators of their own stories. And the lens for this history is often an Indigenous and Black diasporan. The artist Jamea Richmond-Edwards captures for viewers the visual culture and value of Black Detroit around the second millennium, and, as the city undergoes a neocolonialism through neoliberal politics post 2014 bankruptcy, Richmond-Edwards's paintings and collages are relics of a recent past that is becoming more and more distant.

In the early aughts of her art-making career, Richmond-Edwards was committed to rendering portraits of young women and girls she grew up with in 1990s Detroit. Particularly, the artist braided these figures into a narrative of "booster culture," a 1990s neologism describing an economic scheme where a person steals or "boosts" merchandise from retail stores, to sell at a lower price at unregulated (black) markets, usually on the street, in nail salons, or in barbershops. For her 2018 exhibition *Fly Girl Fly*, Richmond-Edwards rendered a series of women in gray skin tone, adorned in colorful garb, furnished through collaged textiles and animated paint colors. One work included in the exhibition, *Archetype of a 5 Star* (2018, p. 14), embodies the style of a Detroit *city girl*, with a range of various textiles, donning a stern face, braided hair, tilted head, hand on hip, and a bent elbow where a monogrammed Givenchy bag is carried as if the subject is giving a formal presentation on it. *Archetype of a 5 Star* is not unlike the British "Grand Manner" or "Grand Style" portraits of the eighteenth century, in which royal aristocrats are rendered in formal attire and adorned in their finest wardrobe and accessories, to convey their dignified status and wealth.[5] *Archetype of a 5 Star*, taking its name from Yo Gotti and Nicki Minaj's "5 Star" 2009 hip-hop hit, suggests one's own insistence on establishing themselves within an economic hierarchy through the form of dress, and access to material culture, even if they may not come from wealth. It is this material culture that enables a fabula-

3 "The Fugitive Slave Act of 1850 ensured that even if 'runaway' slaves arrived in free states in the North, they could be captured and sent back to the slave holders. However, Canada, which lay only one mile across the Detroit River, prohibited slavery, offering full liberation and safety." See "Underground Railroad," Encyclopedia of Detroit, Detroit Historical Society, accessed June 15, 2023, https://detroithistorical.org/learn/encyclopedia-of-detroit/underground-railroad#:~:text=Detroit%2C%20codenamed%20%E2%80%9CMidnight%2C%E2%80%9D,back%20to%20the%20slave%20holders.

4 Michael Gerstein, "Michigan's First 'Sanctuary City' Sparks Anger, Praise," *Detroit News*, April 5, 2017, https://www.detroitnews.com/story/news/politics/2017/04/05/michigans-first-sanctuary-city-sparks-anger-praise/100095900/.

5 "British and American Grand Manner Portraits of the 1700s," National Gallery of Art, Washington, DC, accessed June 15, 2023, https://www.nga.gov/features/slideshows/british-and-american-grand-manner-portraits-of-the-1700s.html.

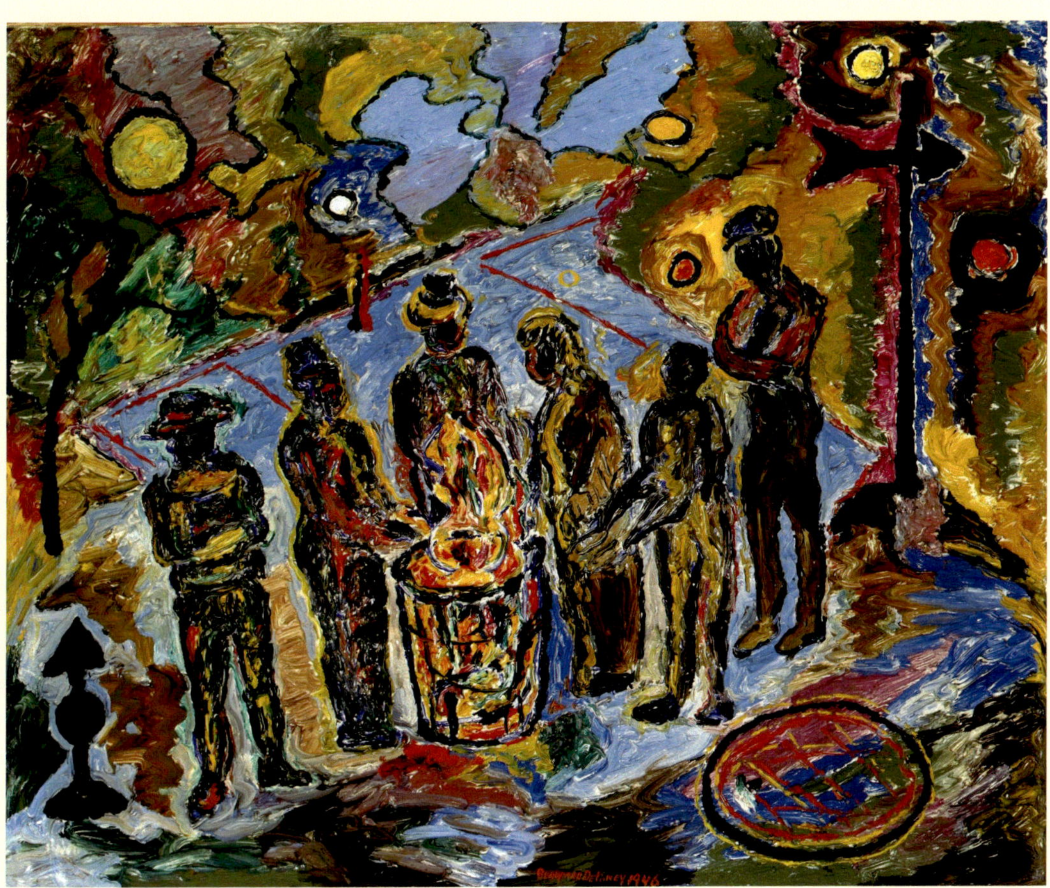

Beauford Delaney, CAN FIRE IN THE PARK, 1946
Oil on canvas
24 × 30 in.
Smithsonian American Art Museum, Museum purchase, 1989.23

tion toward the good life. This way of accessing luxury goods through boosted means allowed working-class individuals to skirt mass wealth accumulation, all while associating themselves within a certain class structure through small material goods, even if they may belong to a lineage of subjugation.

Works from this series established the consistency of Richmond-Edwards's color palette, which included bright vibrant hues and textures inspired by Coogi sweaters, known for their curvy, vertical knitted lines of various colors that create an embossed effect reminiscent of the heavy impasto style of Beauford Delaney portraits such as *Can Fire in the Park* (1946, above). "Stink pink" alligator-skin shoes were common in the Midwest to accompany prom and graduation suits among men. And likewise, women wore crocheted GiGi Hunter dresses that often took the form of halter tops and miniskirts—to be worn on Belle Isle and at cookouts during the few months when it was hot in the city. These brands, along with Guess denim jacket suits, Gucci loafers, and designer baguettes worn off the cuff or over the shoulder, as well as Cartier glasses, were coveted and aspirational to young Black Detroiters in this era. Richmond-Edwards also credits much of her color palette to the African Commune of Bad Relevant Artists (AfriCOBRA) movement, born out of Chicago in 1968, which incorporated bright colors and warped text to fabricate images of Black power and transcendence. The artist studied at Howard University, where AfriCOBRA founder Jeff Donaldson was a professor in the art department. Howard, a historically Black university, was deeply entrenched in ideologies of Pan-Africanism and self-determination, which likely influenced Richmond-Edwards's work as well. Taking from contemporary art references, Richmond-Edwards studied color theory through the ways in which people in her immediate community would fashion themselves for social events. This visual culture included red leathers with black denim; lavender crocodile-skin shoes with all-white polyester; and baby-blue crocheted dresses with patent heels. There was never such a thing as *too much*; there was always

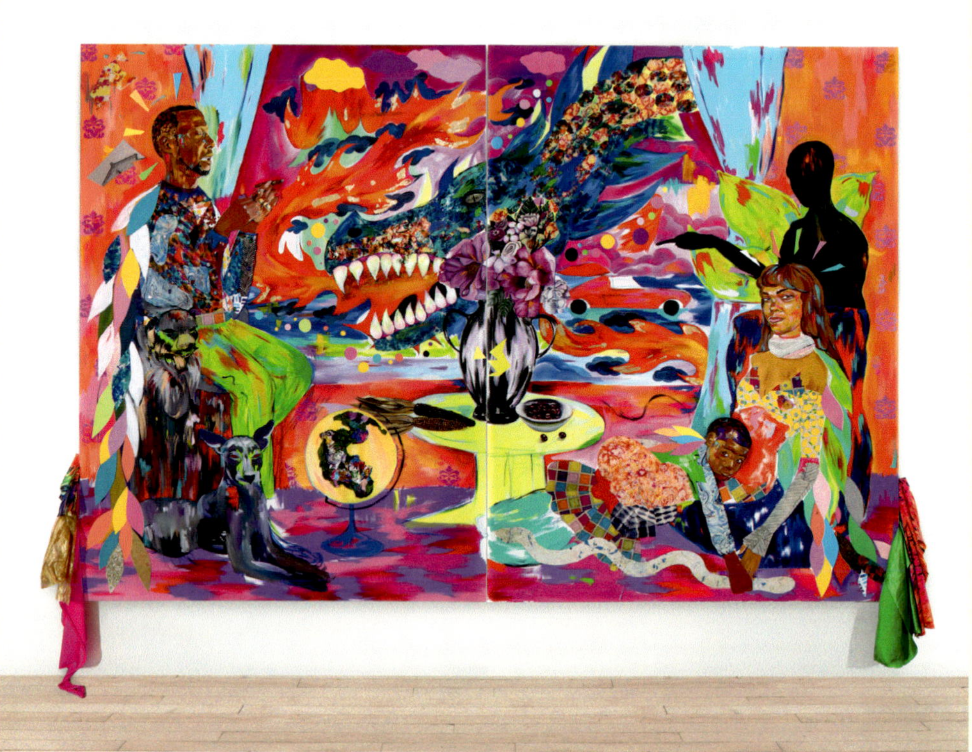

Fire Next Time, 2022
Acrylic, oil pastel, fabric, glitter, rhinestones, gold leaf, and mixed-media collage on canvas
96 × 144 in.

an occasion for excess in "the good life." As Zora Neale Hurston has declared, "Every phase of Negro life is highly dramatised. No matter how joyful or how sad the case there is sufficient poise for drama. Everything is acted out. Unconsciously for the most part of course. There is an impromptu ceremony always ready for every hour of life. No little moment passes unadorned."[6]

While Richmond-Edwards still employs the vibrant color and texture palettes of her previous work, the subject matter has changed from studies of broader trends of value ascription and aspirations, to how value is being defined within her own genealogy and inheritance. Since 2022—which also marked her reverse migration back to Detroit from Mississippi after living in the South for several years—Richmond-Edwards conducted extensive genealogy research of more than seven generations back in her ancestry. In doing so, the artist discovered that her ancestors had atypical experiences in the Black American context; they were entrepreneurs and landowners; they lived in and possibly originated from Europe; and they appeared to skirt around the pervasive racial violence and economic disenfranchisement that most African Americans experienced prior to the civil rights era. This new information provided a new lens for the artist in viewing and understanding recent trauma and loss within her family. This history became a source of empowerment. This new suite of paintings offers a way for the artist to lament family members and the "communal practices of survival"[7] that were often imminent for Black Americans in Detroit. The artist has found great peace and pride in learning about the success of her predecessors and how that success can be engendered for future generations. In addition, the artist braids broader historical narratives of triumph over colonization with futurity and myth making.

Also informing the artist's recent shift in subject matter is a spiritual encounter that happened in 2022. In that year, Richmond-Edwards began recalling family lore that was told to her throughout her life about elders

6 Zora Neale Hurston, *"Characteristics of Negro Expression," in Negro: An Anthology*, ed. Nancy Cunard (London: Nancy Cunard at Wishart, 1934), 24.

7 Aimee Meredith Cox, *Shapeshifters: Black Girls and the Choreography of Citizenship* (Durham, NC: Duke University Press, 2015), 70.

who frequently experienced divine encounters. As a result, Richmond-Edwards began to take up the device of mythos in her visual work to remark about certain interior value systems and inheritances within her own bloodline. With explicit references to ancient Egypt, futurity, Pan-Africanism, and non-Western beliefs, viewers might locate this recent body of work within Afrofuturism, many definitions of which have evolved since writer Mark Dery coined the term in his 1994 essay "Back to the Future." However, it is the definition provided by the film critic Ashley Clark, in relation to his recent selection of Afrofuturist films, which can be ascribed to Richmond-Edwards's work: "centering of the international black experience in alternate and imagined realities, whether fiction or documentary; past or present; science fiction or straight drama."[8] This is most evident in the self-portrait work *The Titans Marched On* (2023), in which the artist has made five versions of herself facing the audience, but turned slightly to the left, with her gaze following the direction of their position, as if the multiple figures are focused on something outside of the left frame of the canvas. Each avatar of the artist is adorned in different headgear; several figures sport headdresses that resemble elaborate hats found in Black churches, whereas the doppelganger in the center of the frame favors a yellow glass dome-like headpiece. The two figures in the foreground hold scepters, and serpent motifs are depicted throughout the colorful scene. The painting betrays time, and appears in an atemporal space of oneness, including two shadow figures flanked in the center of the gathering, indicating a connection to clandestine forces. Richmond-Edwards's mythos paintings elicit an imaginary world that is not bound by time, which engages ancestors who have passed on, in addition to living beings and multiple selves. These works gesture to remark about supernatural encounters. Recurring spiritual symbols exist throughout these paintings, such as orbs—spherical forms that represent connections with the spirit world—and serpents and dragons, which, through an African spirituality lens, indicate a certain relationship to prowess and power. Beyond the device of material culture, these works suggest that the use of metaphysical and ancestral tools may ensure a *good life*. As many African traditional religions establish, acknowledging and praising elders who came before can elicit prosperity and success in this realm.

Recently on view in Detroit, in an exhibition entitled *Currency*, in 2022, was *The Fire Next Time* (2022, p. 18), made with acrylic, oil pastel, fabric, glitter, rhinestones, and gold leaf. In it, Richmond-Edwards has created a family portrait, including an image of her husband, who appears to be in a trance or in meditation. The male figure is seated near two large tesems, ancient dog breeds often rendered in ancient Egyptian visual culture. The artist's likeness is displayed on the right-hand side of the composition; her figure consoles a young boy (presumably one of her sons) and she gazes assuredly at the viewer with a slight smirk. A silhouetted shadow figure is placed in the background, cast behind the artist. The central figure in the painting-collage is a large dragon, emitting fire. Despite the seemingly terse scene, all figures appear at peace, sitting around

8 Ashley Clark, "Afrofuturism on Film: Five of the Best," *Film* (blog), *The Guardian*, April 2, 2015, https://www.theguardian.com/film/filmblog/2015/apr/02/afrofuturism-on-film-five-best-brooklyn-bamcinematek.

an altar-like table in the center, bearing two corn husks, a Greco-Roman two-handed vessel housing lavender flowers, and, next to it, palm nuts spilling out of a small white cup. Serpents are covertly displayed throughout; the young boy holds a small serpent in his hand like a sword as he lies on the matriarch figure, whose hand is also on the serpent, suggesting a baton-passing of power and inheritance. In an amalgam of African diasporan, ancient Egyptian, and Greco-Roman symbolism and spirituality, the composition suggests a renewal, an abundance, and a familial agency, as ashes and embers burn, and new life is formed.

In another work, the narrative and myth making becomes more defined. In *Lullaby for a Shooting Star* (2023, p. 40), the artist's avatar is present again; this time, the figure sits on a throne. Several small men on small horses stand at attention, with their profiles displayed, on the left of the painting. The artist's avatar dwarfs the horsemen as her royal figure occupies the entire right side of the work. The composition features the Nancy Brown Peace Carillon monument located on Belle Isle, a small island nestled between Detroit and the Canadian border. *Lullaby for a Shooting Star* was made intuitively by the artist. Without much pretense, the artist rendered a painting that she retroactively understood as a monument to Indigenous Shawnee leader and warrior Tecumseh. Tecumseh, whose name means "Shooting Star," was a leader of the Shawnee tribe who led Indigenous people of all tribes to collaborate with the British in defense of Native lands against US settlers in a battle of the War of 1812. The battle, with Tecumseh's leadership, led to the establishment of then Canadian territory.[9]

In Katherine McKittrick's musings on Detroit's sonic geography, she suggests, "certain buildings are evidence of our geological understanding of space."[10] When I look at *Lullaby for a Shooting Star*, I am reminded of the architecture in Detroit, and the way these historic landmarks may (in addition to historical motifs from the African continent) be informing Richmond-Edwards's composition style in these recent works. For instance, one of Detroit's most beloved structures that is akin to Richmond-Edwards's visual style is the forty-story Art Deco Guardian Building. One of the city's first skyscrapers, situated a few streets from the Detroit River that separates the US–Canadian border, it is indicative of the pre–Great Depression era. It reflects grandeur, and the celebration of the industrial boom of the 1920s, although it was erected on the brink of the 1930s Depression. The building is known for its custom tangerine brick exterior and vibrantly colored interior, which includes a cathedral-like terra-cotta mural of Michigan and its industries, with a holy figure in the center. The mural incorporates Aztec and Native American design, and was executed by designer Ezra Winter.

The building, originally designed for a bank by architect Wirt Rowland, is more like a cathedral than an

9 Tecumseh was known for his organizing among Indigenous people, and, despite a general desire for tribalism among Natives in the region, was fierce in his organizing for a Pan-Nativist unification to defeat common enemies. See Gregory Evans Dowd, *A Spirited Resistance: The North American Indian Struggle for Unity, 1745–1815* (Baltimore: Johns Hopkins University Press, 1993).

10 "Katherine McKittrick, a conversation on Black Dreamcatchers," interview by Ryan Clarke, February 2023, *Dweller* (blog), accessed July 7, 2023, https://dweller-forever.blog/2023/05/katherine-mckittrick-a-conversation-on-black-dreamcatchers.

office building. It offers up several areas of spiritual contemplation and expansively colorful renderings. Richmond-Edwards's work is indirectly informed by these nineteenth- and twentieth-century histories of architecture, with origins that are often spiritually led, in a desire for unification, peace, and freedom, with a subtext rooted in nation-state ideologies and coloniality. This and other monuments to the postindustrial age, innovation, invention, and, by the twentieth century, a relatively new country, America, represent a future outlook on who and what Detroit was made for. As Black Americans migrated from Southern cities to be exploited in factories for the benefit of larger corporations and banks, it is safe to assume that creative visions imbued onto Detroit by many architects and designers of this booming town in the Fordian age did not consider Black Detroiters as their primary audience. And yet, by the later part of the twentieth century, these spaces became primarily inhabited by Black Detroiters.[11] *How do subjugated classes and oppressed groups gesture toward a good life, when the environments in which they occupy do not consider them?*

While modern Detroit was not made in a vision to accommodate Black Americans, Black Detroiters assume a certain autonomy and fierce protection over its land, diverse ethnic contributions, and creative legacies. Richmond-Edwards's work indexes the lineage of land development, and the terse tribulations and triumphs between white colonists, natives, and Black inhabitants that continue to persist today. Her works also become more a revisionist effort to write in the lives and aspirations of Indigenous and Black residents who weren't considered in the foundations of Detroit's modern making. The artist draws on spiritual phenomena, imagining a new world beyond the limits of one's surroundings.[12] The works indirectly invoke histories of Black Americans' engagement with the divine and outer space, and an escapism to the cosmos. Through these pivots, Richmond-Edwards's *good life* is made manifest through one's relationship to both material objects and deeply seeded connections to family and metaphysical realms. "Good Life" gestures toward another world that was imperceptible to those who were not in and of it. The "Good Life" captures the general sentiment of many Detroiters living and growing up in Detroit in the final two decades before the end of the millennium. As many viewed it as a space of uninhabitable deterioration and civic failure, for those who stayed, it was a Black American mecca where certain signs and signifiers were championed and ubiquitous in this intersubjective space.

11 In 1956, German architect Ludwig Mies van der Rohe was invited to imagine a residential oasis for white Detroiters who began fleeing the city post World War II, leaving the city primarily inhabited by the Black working class. The historic, primarily African American Black Bottom and Paradise Valley neighborhoods were razed to accommodate Mies van der Rohe's vision, in an effort to retain the city's declining white tax base. See "Mies van der Rohe Residential District, Lafayette Park," Encyclopedia of Detroit, Detroit Historical Society, accessed July 12, 2023, https://detroithistorical.org/learn/encyclopedia-of-detroit/mies-van-der-rohe-residential-district-lafayette-park.

12 Aimee Meredith Cox has written about how geography determines one's proximity to success and survival in postindustrial Detroit: "race as historically and spatially formed determines who is both deemed valueless and identified as a future failure." See Cox, *Shapeshifters*, 69.

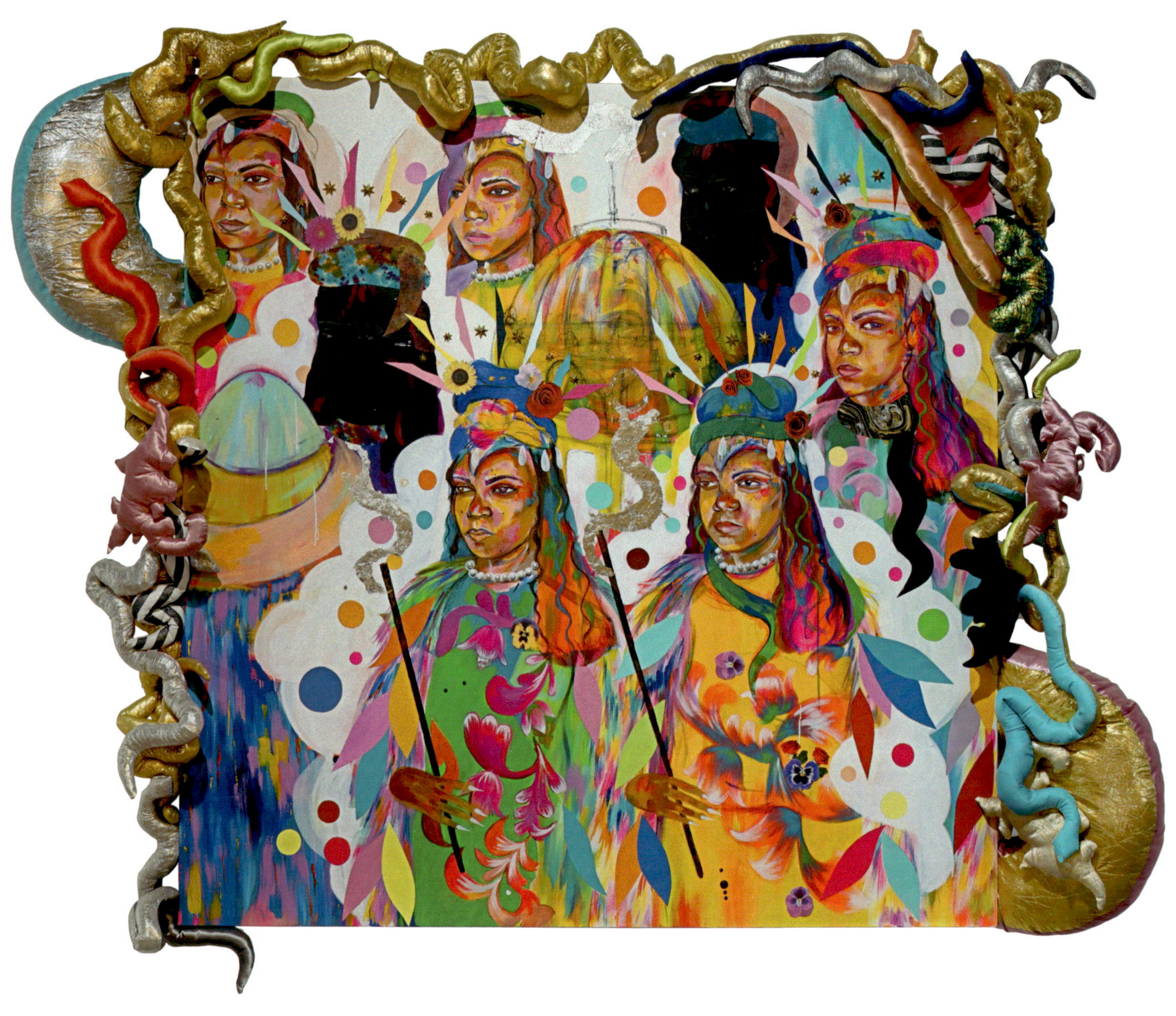

March of the Nagas, 2023
Acrylic, silver leaf, rhinestones, glitter, mixed-media collage,
and soft sculpture on canvas
72 × 72 in.

CONJURING A SOVEREIGN REIGN

NIAMA SAFIA SANDY

In Fall 1971, James Baldwin and Nikki Giovanni met in London for a now iconic interview. Among the many resonant statements made during the course of their conversation, James Baldwin said:

> Now when our game starts running. And after all, baby, after all, we have survived the roughest game in the history of the world. You know we really have. No matter what we say against ourselves. No matter what our limits, our hang ups are, we have come through something. And if we can get this far, we can get further. And we got this far by means no one understands—including you and me. We're only beginning to apprehend it. And you're a poet precisely because you are beginning to apprehend it and put it into a form that will be useful for your kid, and his kid, and for the world because we're not obliged to accept the world's definitions.[1]

We don't need to conjecture about what Baldwin meant by "the roughest game in the history of the world," but for the sake of clarity, my reading of it extends to the totality of epistemology and the post-Enlightenment evidence-based observable Western histories we have come to accept. Yes, he could be talking about the narrative of the blight of the transatlantic slave trade and the unanticipated beauty and power Black people have created through it and its afterlives in the Americas and beyond. Baldwin lived through some of the most fascinating and disturbing periods in recent global history. Born in Harlem at the height of the New Negro movement (or the Harlem Renaissance, as most of us know it), he came of age during the end of World War II, and into his own as a novelist and public intellectual at the height of the Civil Rights Movement in the 1950s. He died in 1987, during the midpoint of the crack epidemic, the rise of hip-hop culture into the mainstream, the denouement of the Reagan era, and much more. He wrote, loved, and lived prolifically. He saw it all and one could argue that he predicted what he didn't directly observe.

We know about the often-discussed pathologies of the West as they relate to the tolls they have exercised and excised on Black life. In the face of what has certainly been the most disturbing period of my relatively young life, many Black artists and creative practitioners are making work in consideration of what was before that and what can come next despite it. To use Baldwin's metaphor again, what if the game is more ancient and contains far more forgotten knowledge rended from history than even what is known and observable now? And what's more, what if we can win it? It opens the door to the notion of "knowing" encompassing a networked, speculative methodology that can invite us to feel, heal, intuit, imagine, and think expansively toward that which will bring us closer to the version of freedom our ancestors might have imagined. In the last decade, I have closely read and been jarred by the work of several artists across disciplines who I feel offer us a gateway and themselves strongly embody this idea. I am beginning to understand that they are the next wave that may be the push toward us getting "our game

1 *Soul!*, episode 53, "Nikki Giovanni and James Baldwin in Conversation (Part 1)," produced by Ellis Haizlip, aired December 15, 1971, on WNET, YouTube video, 58:13, https://www.youtube.com/watch?v=AFGkNEt30Fo.

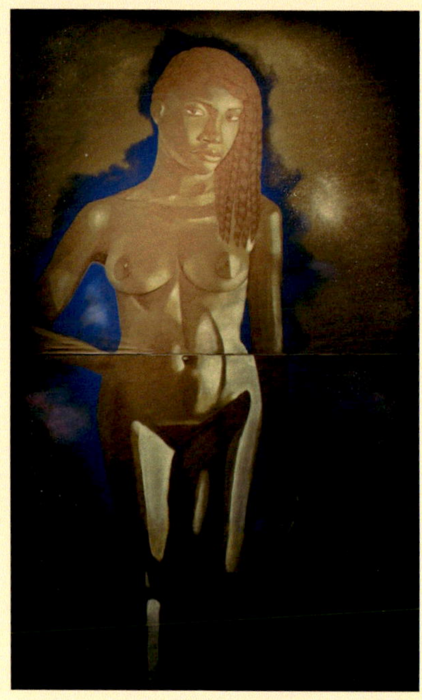

CONSEQUENTLY VULNERABLE
(diptych), 2014
Ink and chalk pastel on board
80 × 32 in.

running." The work of Jamea Richmond-Edwards, through its generative core processes, color palette, and the ontological space it beckons us to enter, represents an instantiation of a framework that pulses us toward reclaiming the fullness of our power.

I met Richmond-Edwards for the first time at Prizm Art Fair in Miami in December 2016. It was a Friday afternoon, on a sweltering Miami day, in an even more sweltering warehouse in Little Haiti. Along with another artist on the panel and other artists in the audience, she was in conversation about artist collectives. I was on a panel immediately after, so my mind was in a space of keen listening. Her remarks demonstrated an urgent need for a paradigmatic generational shift in contemporary visual arts, akin to the Black Arts Movement. It piqued my interest as slides of her work scrolled on the screen behind her. Her work in that time period was mostly centered on black-and-white drawings of Black women with braided hair adorned with ethereal feathers and clothing collaged from carefully hand-dyed cut paper and recycled artworks, often on richly colored backgrounds. She specifically invoked AfriCOBRA, the African Commune of Bad Relevant Artists. Founded on the Southside of Chicago in 1968 by Jeff Donaldson, Wadsworth Jarrell, Jae Jarrell, Barbara Jones-Hogu, Gerald Williams, and others, the group proposed a visual language that could "revolutionize art by presenting compositionally solid, informative, and conceptually revolutionary art that comprised African American communities, with us having ownership of our ideas."[2] The school of thought, which initially called itself COBRA,[3] asserted precepts that would guide the work of its members. Founding member Jeff Donaldson asserted in a 1970 manifesto that the collective's works would offer "intelligent definition of the past, and perceptive identification in the present" while projecting "nationfull direction in the future."[4] Members' work abided by notions of expression of African Diasporic or African American experience and positionality, rhythm, and symmetry "based on African music and African movement," "organic looking, [and] feeling forms," where mimesis, the real, and "the overreal" meet, shine, and color.[5]

After completing undergraduate studies at Jackson State University, the artist received graduate training under the tutelage of Ron Akili Anderson, an AfriCOBRA member, at Howard University. Inspired by Anderson,

2 Wadsworth A. Jarrell, "Introduction," in *AfriCOBRA: Experimental Art toward a School of Thought* (Durham, NC: Duke University Press, 2020), 7.

3 Not to be confused with the avant-garde CoBrA collective established in Europe in 1948. CoBrA stands for *Co*penhagen, *Br*ussels, and *A*msterdam, hotbeds of artistic activity in the postwar period.

4 Jeff Donaldson, "10 in Search of a Nation," n.p. Jeff Donaldson papers, 1918–2005, bulk 1960s–2005, Archives of American Art, Smithsonian Institution.

5 Ibid.

Donaldson, and others, the extensions of the group's methodologies were then, and still are, clearly present in her work. Rather than the focus on the general Black American experience AfriCOBRA advocated for, Richmond-Edwards has often focused on representing Black women, specifically and almost exclusively, considering them a nexus for the creation of the world as we know it (and perhaps as we don't)—both literally and figuratively. There is energy, channeled through the artist's hand, and a collective energy offered and transmuted through her use of recycled artworks.

Some months after our initial introduction, I finally encountered Richmond-Edwards's work in person in a solo exhibition at Long-Sharp Gallery in New York. One work in particular, *Consequently Vulnerable* (2014), called to me. The diptych tableau featured a nude female figure drawn with black paper and black ink. She looked as though she was almost floating in the cosmos. I read her as gliding through the stars—not aimless, but in exploration. She was beyond gravity, unfettered by any other constraints of what we understand to be the rules that govern interstellar space. She was not following an orbit predetermined by any other force but her own will. It seemed to me that she was a planet, perhaps even a galaxy, unto herself, charged enough to create whatever future outcome she desired. The artist has said of the piece:

> This is the only nude I've ever made. I don't even remember making this body of work. It was from spirit, I was a vessel for many things. But when I look at that work, at the time I was looking at my relationship or my experience with womanhood, being a mother, everything I was going through in the art world, being extremely vulnerable. I thought, what happens if I strip myself, allow myself to be really vulnerable? Because I try to put on a really strong front ...When I look at this work, I'm thinking about...Black women as the nexus of life...melanin, literally Blackness...and it literally being a vessel for the ancestors.[6]

At the time, I was selecting artworks for a second iteration of my debut series of exhibitions, *Black Magic: AfroPasts/AfroFutures*, at Honfleur Gallery in Washington, DC. The exhibition series posited Afrofuturism and magic realism as nodal points on a continuum of global Black Diasporic creative and spiritual expressions as tools for survival. The terms speak to something beyond mere aesthetics, toward an ambulatory cosmology. I invited artists whose practices sit at the intersections of the past, present, and future, grounded in the "half lives" (after an idea posited by Christina Sharpe) of the "psychic and physical remnants of our ancestors" in the atmosphere.[7] I was interested in how their strategies might help the artists shape themselves and the world. I knew immediately that *Consequently Vulnerable* had to be included.

6 "Black Magic: AfroPasts/AfroFutures," artist talk with Adrienne Gaither, Charles Jean-Pierre, Jamea Richmond-Edwards, and Danny Simmons, moderated by Niama Safia Sandy, Honfleur Gallery, Washington, DC, September 16, 2017.

7 Sharpe has theorized that "the past that is not past reappears, always, to rupture the present." In the same book, quoting a poem by Dionne Brand, she offers the imperative of breath to be drawn "with wonder and admiration . . . like hydrogen, like oxygen." See Christina Sharpe, *In the Wake: On Blackness and Being* (Durham, NC: Duke University Press, 2016), 9, 109. In chemistry, half-life refers to the time taken for one-half of an element to decay. In 2017, joining these ideas, I posited that our ancestors—including those who chose to find freedom by giving themselves to the sea—have become particulate, constituent, and constant in the very air we breathe. See my curatorial statement for *Black Magic: AfroPasts/AfroFutures*, Honfleur Gallery, August 19–October 7, 2017.

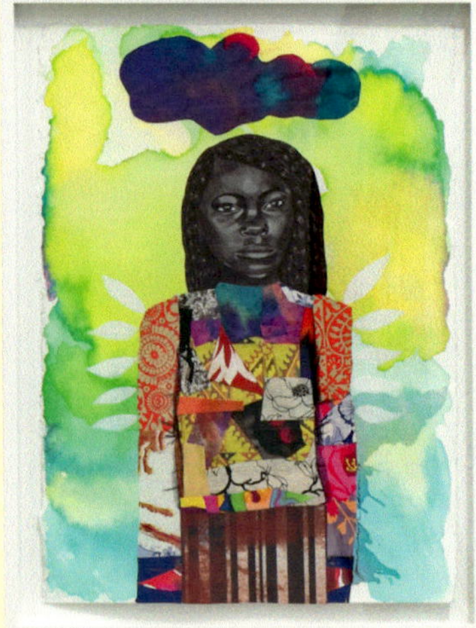
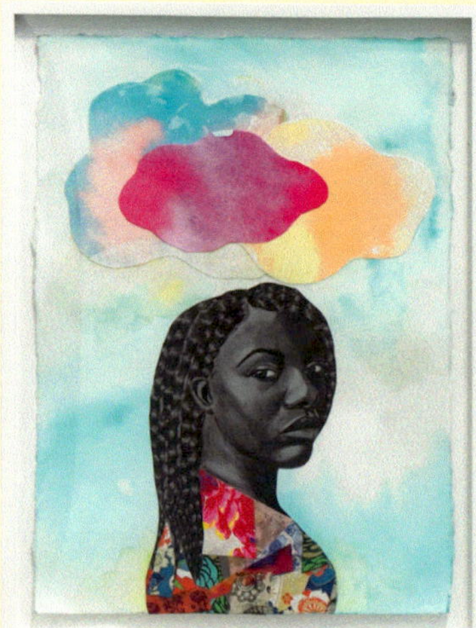
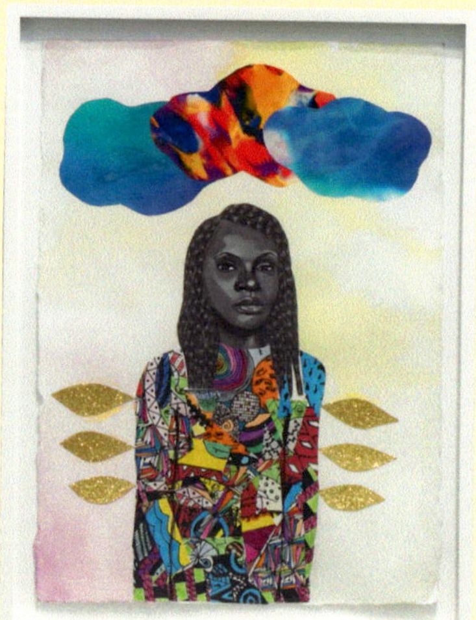

7-Mile Girls 6, 2017
Watercolor, collage, and ink on paper
15 × 11 in.

7-Mile Girls 5, 2017
Watercolor, collage, and ink on paper
15 × 11 in.

7-Mile Girls 4, 2017
Watercolor, collage, and ink on paper
15 × 11 in.

Looking back at the artwork now, I see visual resonances in the black-ink-on-black-paper figure and depictions of the women of ancient Egypt in drawings and sculptures, as well as depictions of the Egyptian deity Nut. She is the goddess of the heavenly bodies and the universe itself, who protects the dead as they enter the afterlife. The goddess was often depicted naked, stretching her blue-black star-spangled body across the expanse of the sky, or as a cow standing between humans and the chaos of the disordered cosmos. In hindsight, I believe the 2014 mixed-media collage work opened a portal for the artist, allowing her the freedom to call herself and her ancestors to her fully. In a September 2017 artist talk, Richmond-Edwards expressed that she believed she was tapping into a type of collective memory, "creating these images of my ancestors or women I don't know but that I've always been yearning for or subconsciously searching for. And so I feel like my work is always connected to the past and I'm this vessel for them."[8]

That freedom transformed her work—from her subjects themselves to her palette. She was clear that the work was leading toward "being liberated from subjugation economically, politically and socially from white supremacy,"[9] which necessitated unapologetically embracing our stories as they are and imagining what more those stories can tell us. There was 2018's *Fly Girl Fly* and *Prom Night* in 2019, each a celebration of the coming-of-age rites of passage of the high school dance, and young adulthood. She carefully centered the aesthetic and adornment processes that come with that and the reality of the pursuit of luxury goods as a marker for social and economic mobility in the Detroit of her childhood, and in so many other cities. She began incorporating orb-like elements that could just as easily be planets.

The scale grew and the color palette brightened, almost like she was looking with brand-new eyes. A shift began toward a more epic tone; each new work began to feel like installments of the ancient long-form poems that tell a story foundational to a culture's past, present, and future. They read like tomes, each composition another step in building a world to present an unfolding saga through action, allegory, and visions of the lushest landscapes of Earth and beyond. What was being depicted expanded to include references to the Richmond family's Indigenous heritage, and the facts revealed through genealogical research that enslavement was not a blighting presence in the lives of generations of Richmonds. What does knowing that history afford a person? What kind of power can be claimed through that knowledge? The works in *Ancient Future* are a culmination in the artist's vision and desire to build a new canon while shining a light that gives honor and reverence to the pathways that led us there.

8 "Black Magic: AfroPasts/AfroFutures."

9 "Prizm Panels: Contemporary Black Artist Movements: With Jamea Richmond-Edwards | Amber Robles-Gordon," Prizm Art Fair, Miami, December 2, 2016, YouTube video, 45:39, https://www.youtube.com/watch?v=EU8ATRaNnCs.

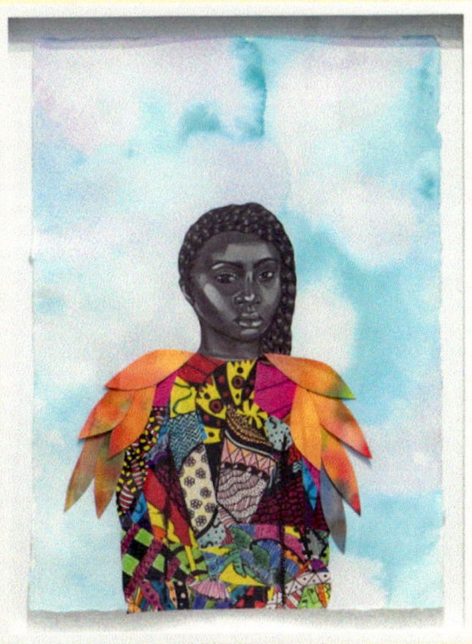

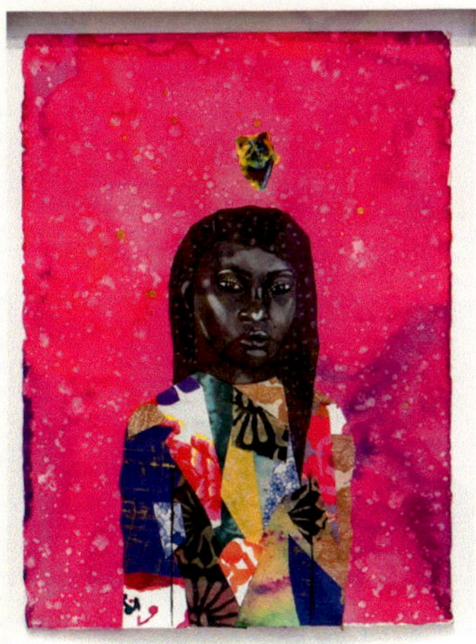

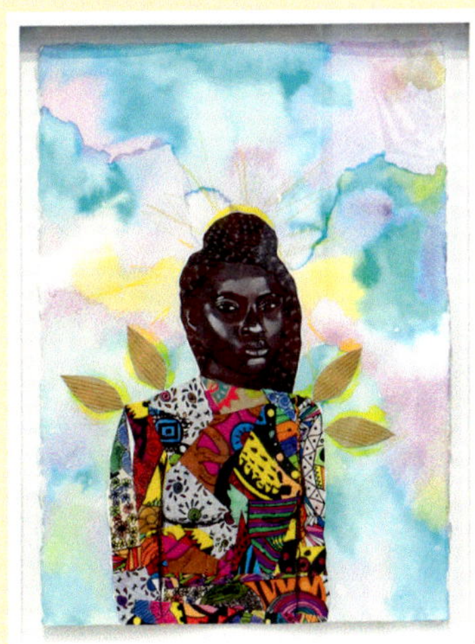

7-Mile Girls 3, 2017
Watercolor, collage, and ink on paper
15 × 11 in.

7-Mile Girls 2, 2017
Watercolor, collage, and ink on paper
15 × 11 in.

7-Mile Girls 1, 2017
Watercolor, collage, and ink on paper
15 × 11 in.

Inspired in part by Donaldson et al.'s use of "cool-ade" colors and the visual references of the pop culture of the artist's youth—*Yo! MTV Raps*, *In Living Color*, hair bubbles, Nerf Super Soakers and footballs, clackers, 8-ball jackets, the pulsating patterns of Coogi sweaters—Richmond-Edwards has reworked the meter of the bright colors and daylight fluorescents of the late 1980s and 1990s into an operating principle. The political terrain was marked by riots in New York and Los Angeles, a 48 percent rise in the population of incarcerated persons,[10] the passing of the 1994 Violent Crime Control and Law Enforcement Act, and countless other incidents that affected the Black community. The palette ranges from warm oranges, pinks, and yellows to cool blues and greens, and purples. While the scenes are not directly depicted, this psychedelic tonality is at once a celebration of the immense pride, pain, and potential of that era and where we find ourselves in the contemporary. The color marks time and feeling, and offers us an opportunity to reexamine the issues of our time with a fresh lens. It's all texture and color, somehow as dense as the heaviest metal and as light as cotton candy. The background colors surge and swirl, taking us on a voyage into a cranked-up answer to the call of the Washington Color School's groundbreaking color field painting style. Instead of using paint alone, Richmond-Edwards evolved her signature seamlessly cut and collaged paper with techniques including airbrush and spray paint to render her landscape scenes.

The composition and coloring of the faces shifted, too. From a figure perspective, they begin to seem more closely modeled on the dimensions and features of the artist's own face, as well as those of family and other loved ones. The color of the faces has shifted to more natural pinks and browns approximate to Black people's natural skin tones. Rendered both in paper and ink, and as soft sculpture breaking out of the picture plane, there are visual invocations of the long-held views of the transformative powers of serpents. New works in *Ancient Future* offer figures in regalia, moving together in phalanx-like formation, harkening back to Richmond-Edwards's time as a French horn player in Jackson State University's renowned Sonic Boom of the South marching band. The black, inky figures appear again, perhaps as her ancestors, descendants, those in her line cast as diviners and the ones who will lead the way to a new history. They are all present, either in formation or in fantastical scenes invoking tales of the ancient Sibyls, renowned women seers of old who were imbued with the gift of divining prophecies of the future. These scenes invite the viewer to consider the place and power that narratives may be enacting in their own lives. *What is a limiting story you have told yourself? How can you claim full sovereignty over your life?*

10 Jenni Gainsborough and Marc Mauer, "Diminishing Returns: Crime and Incarceration in the 1990s" (September 2000), The Sentencing Project, Prison Policy Initiative, https://www.prisonpolicy.org/scans/sp/DimRet.pdf.

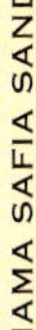

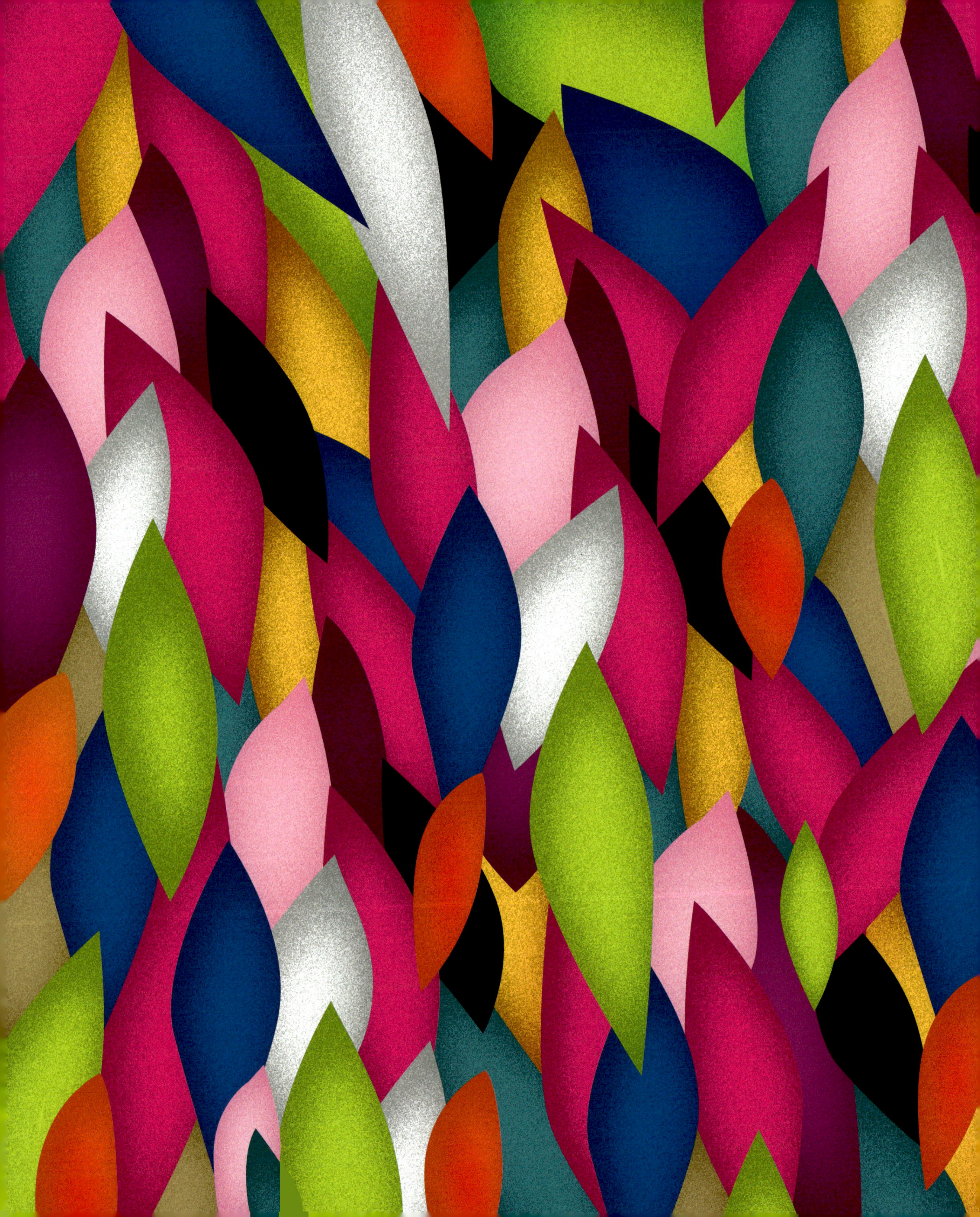

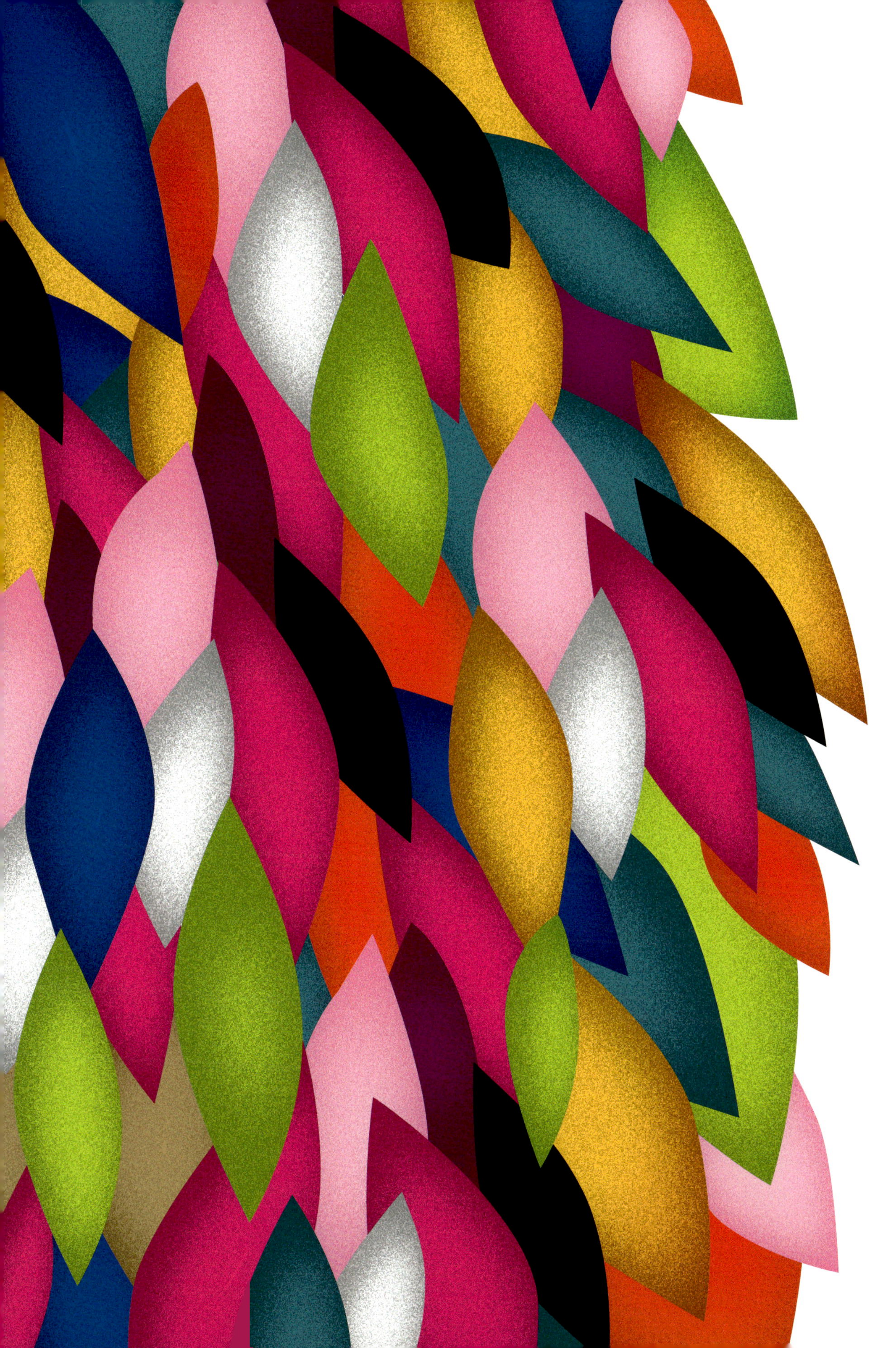

PLATES

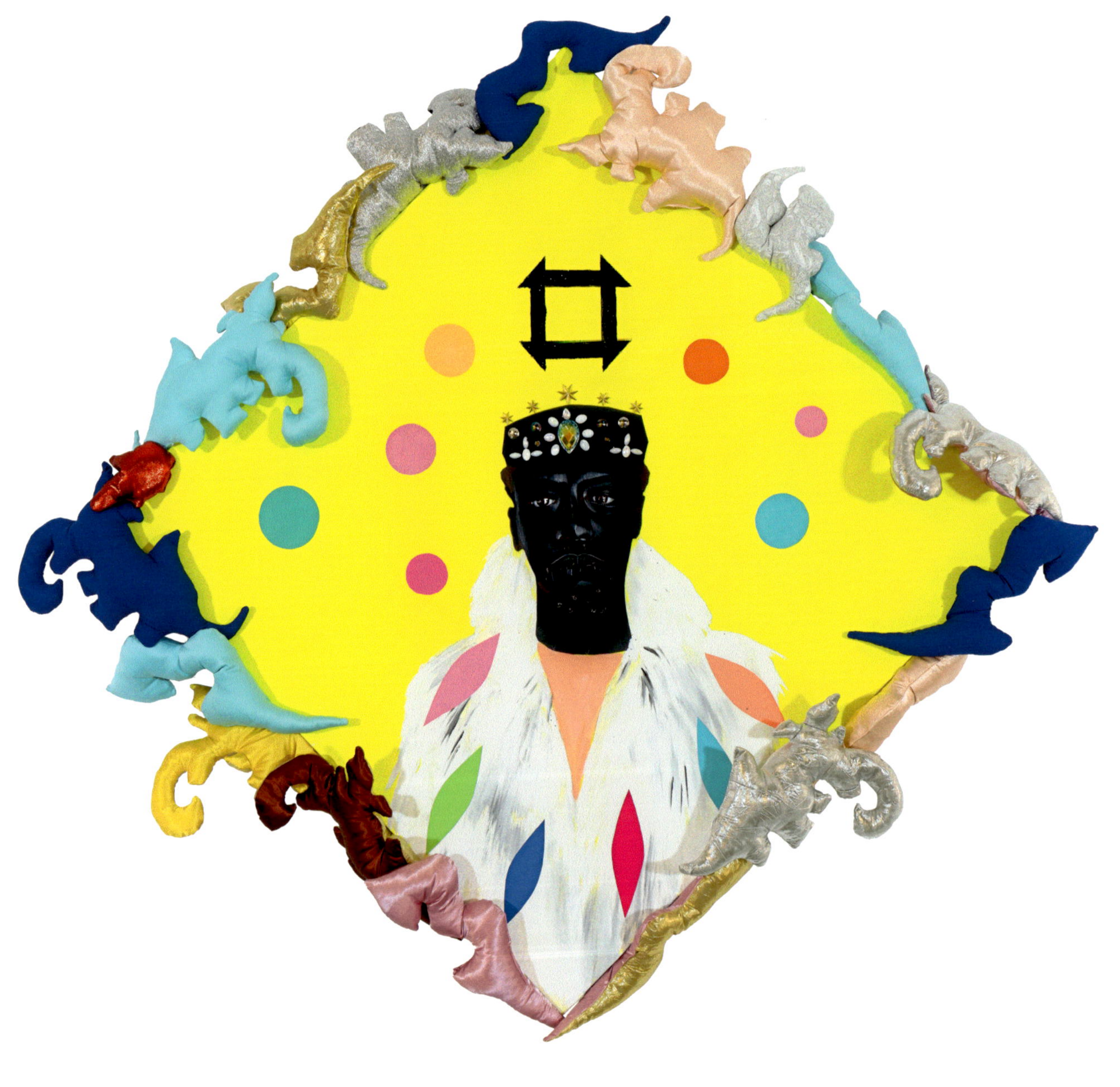

The Man, The Myth, The Legend, 2023
Acrylic, rhinestones, glitter, mixed-media collage,
and soft sculpture on canvas
46 × 46 in.

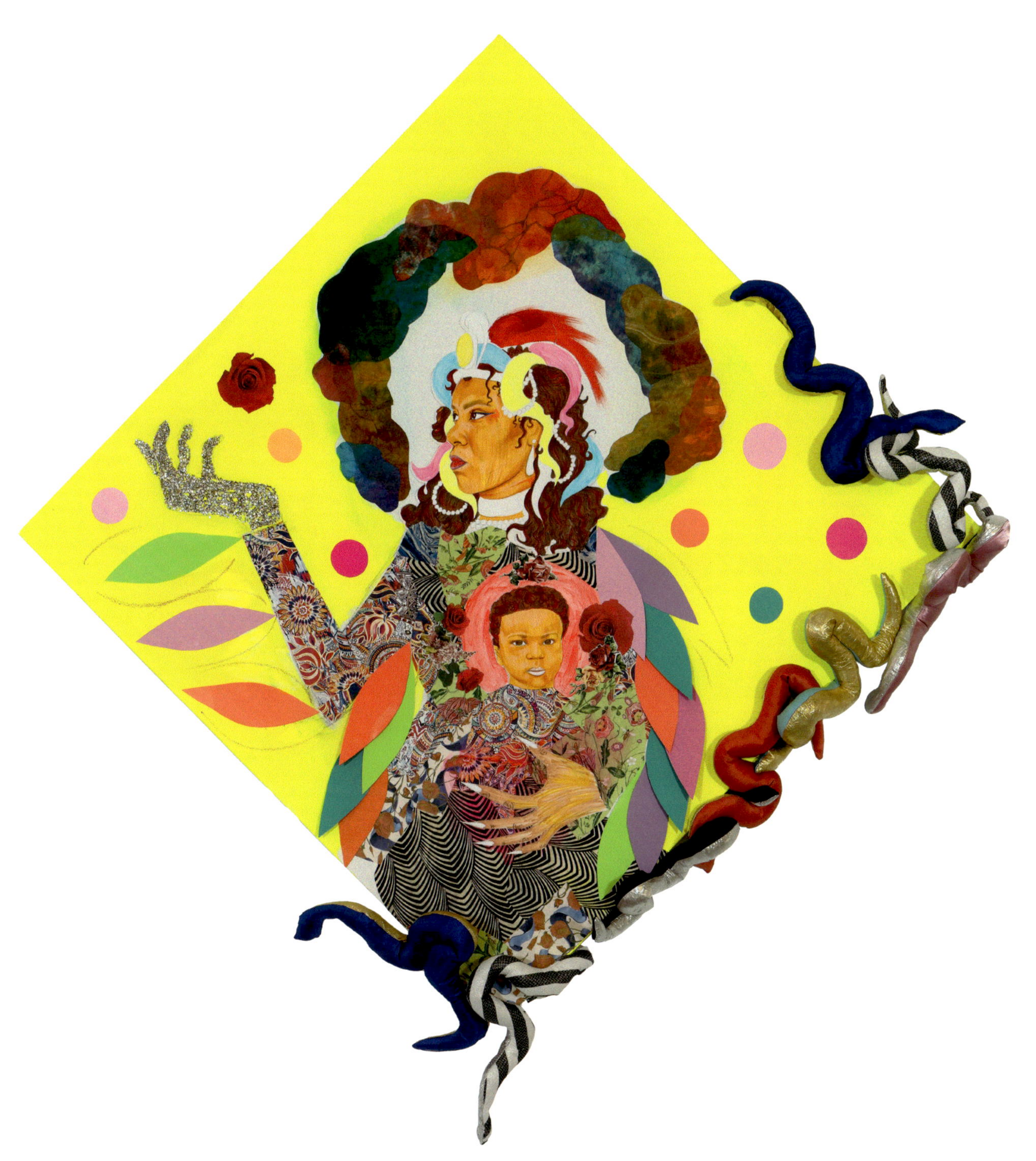

Mother and Child, 2023
Acrylic, gold leaf, glitter, mixed-media collage,
and soft sculpture on canvas
46 × 46 in.

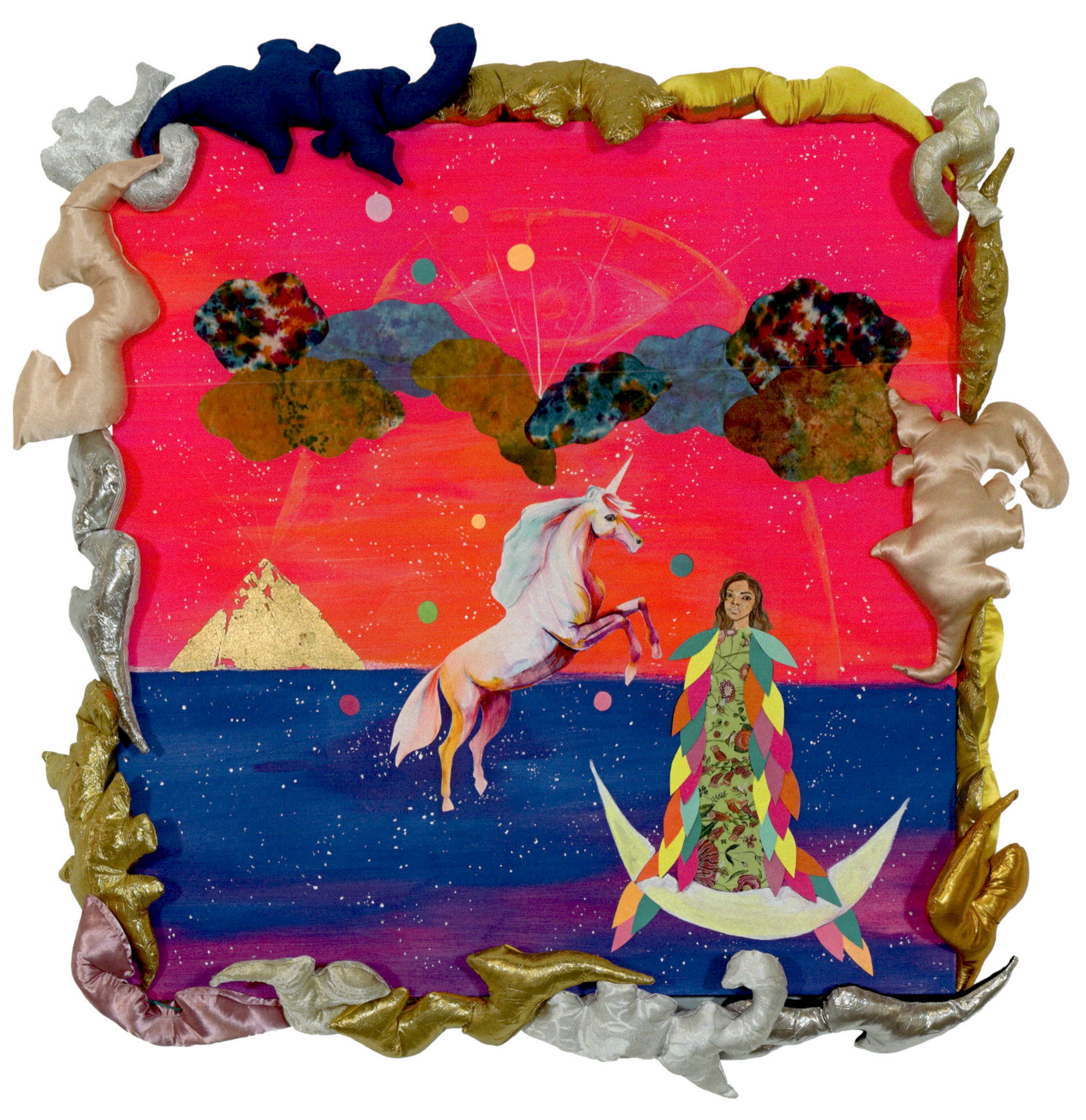

A Girl and Her Unicorn, 2023
Acrylic, gold leaf, glitter, mixed-media collage,
and soft sculpture on canvas
46 × 46 in.

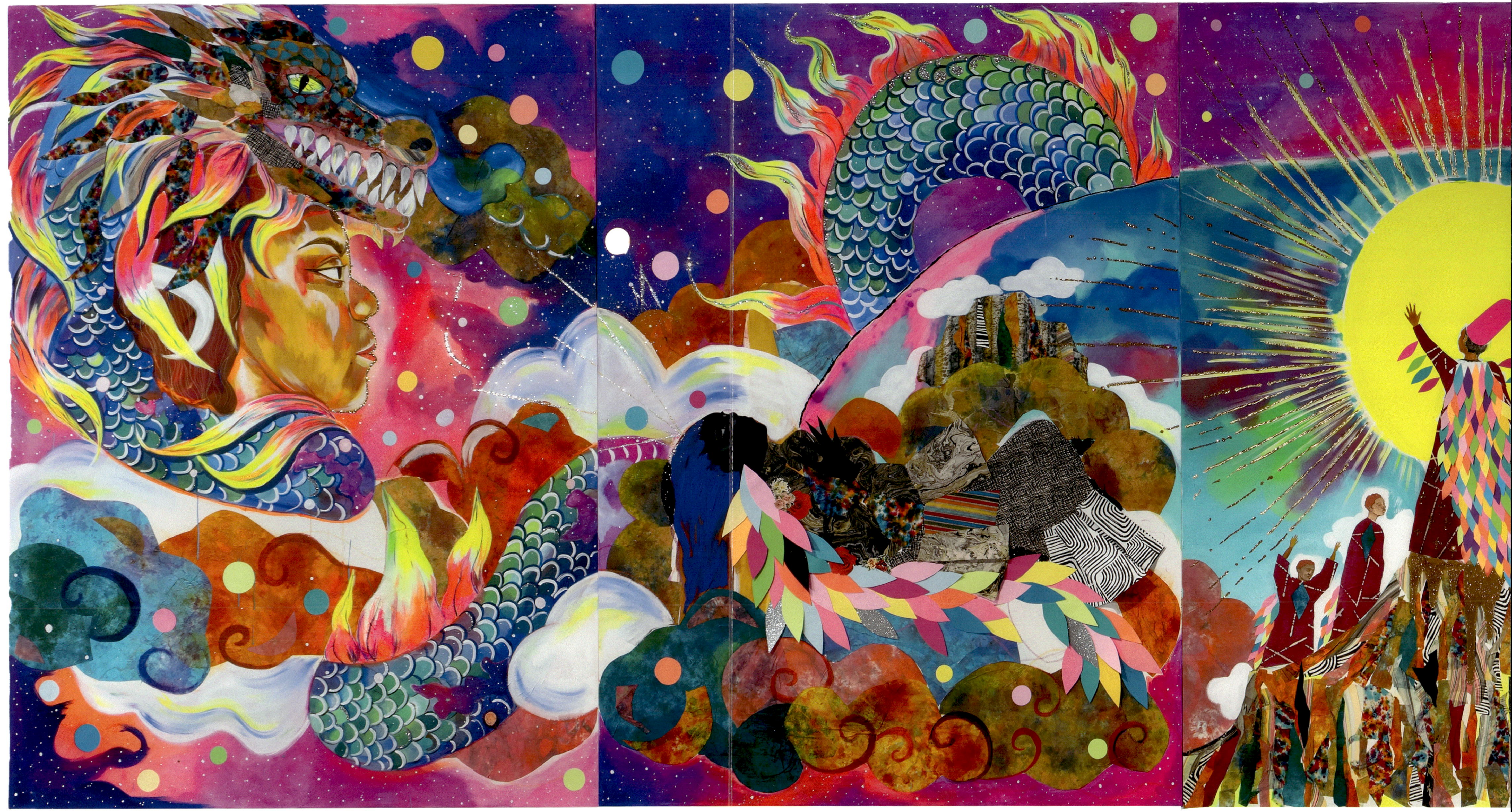

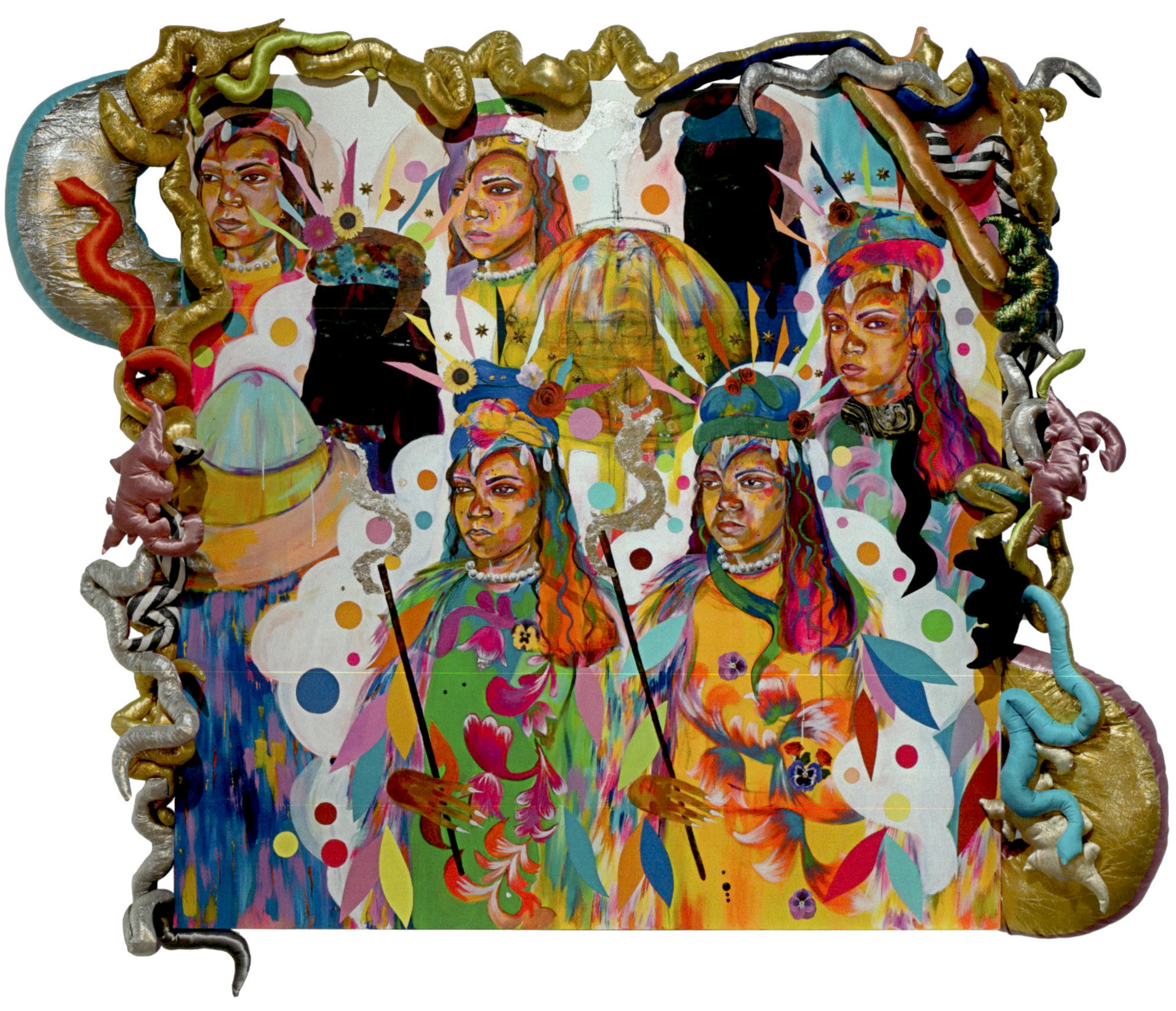
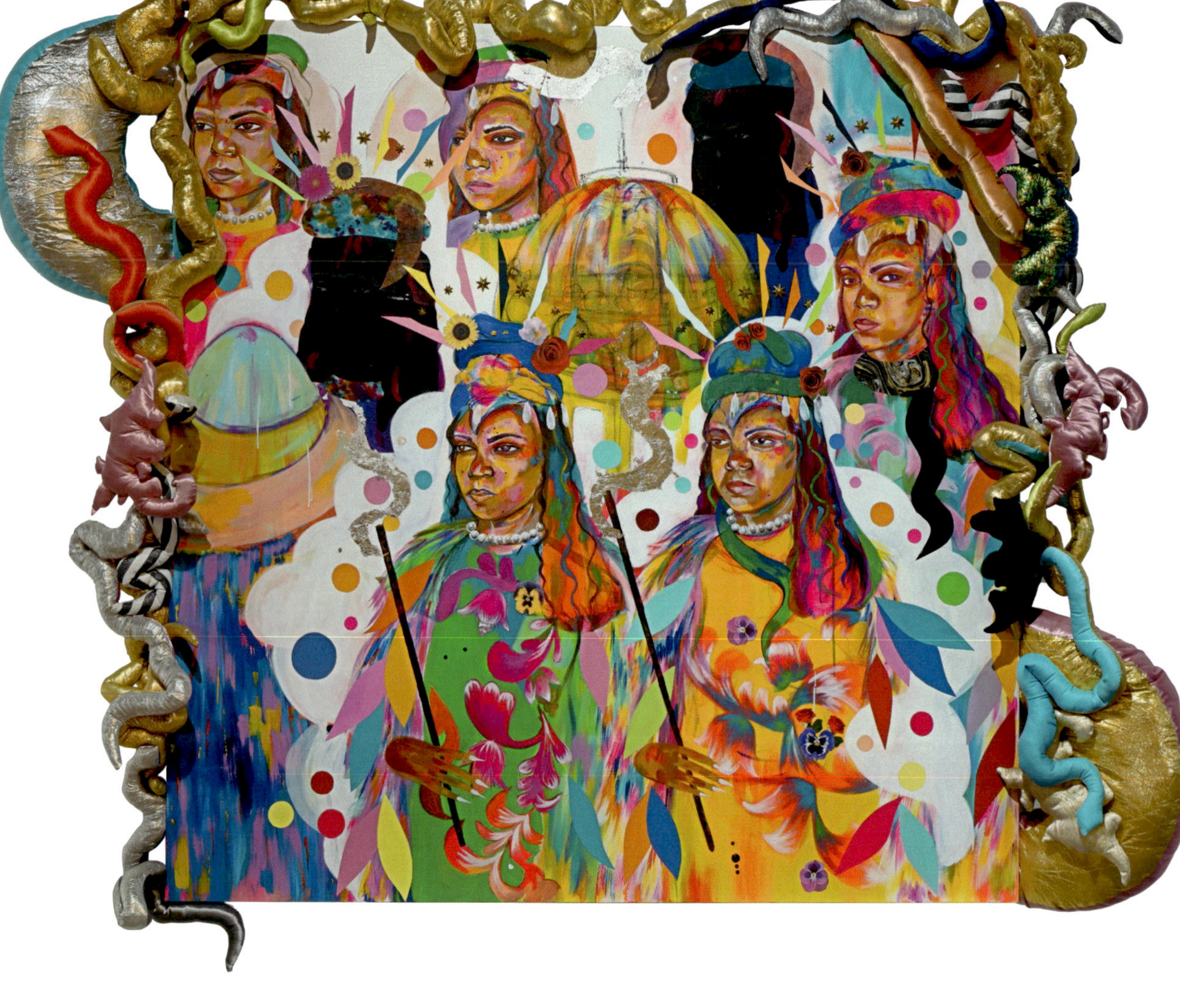

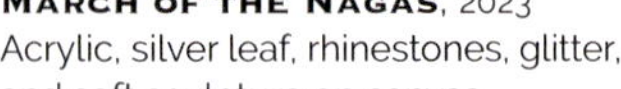
March of the Nagas, 2023
Acrylic, silver leaf, rhinestones, glitter, mixed-media collage, and soft sculpture on canvas
72 × 72 in.

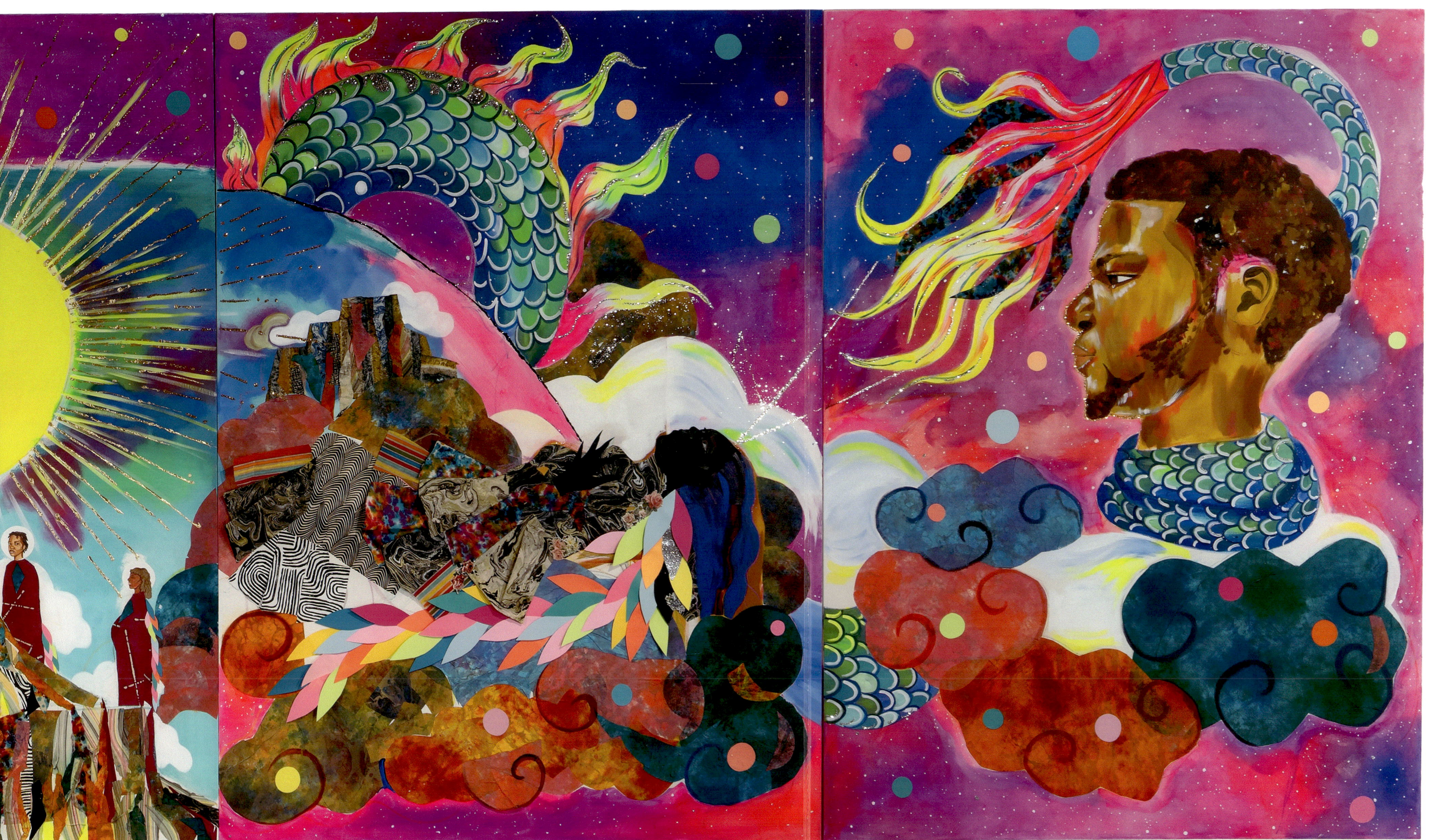

Dark Night of the Soul, 2023
Acrylic, gold leaf, glitter, mixed-media collage, and soft sculpture on canvas
96 × 360 in. overall

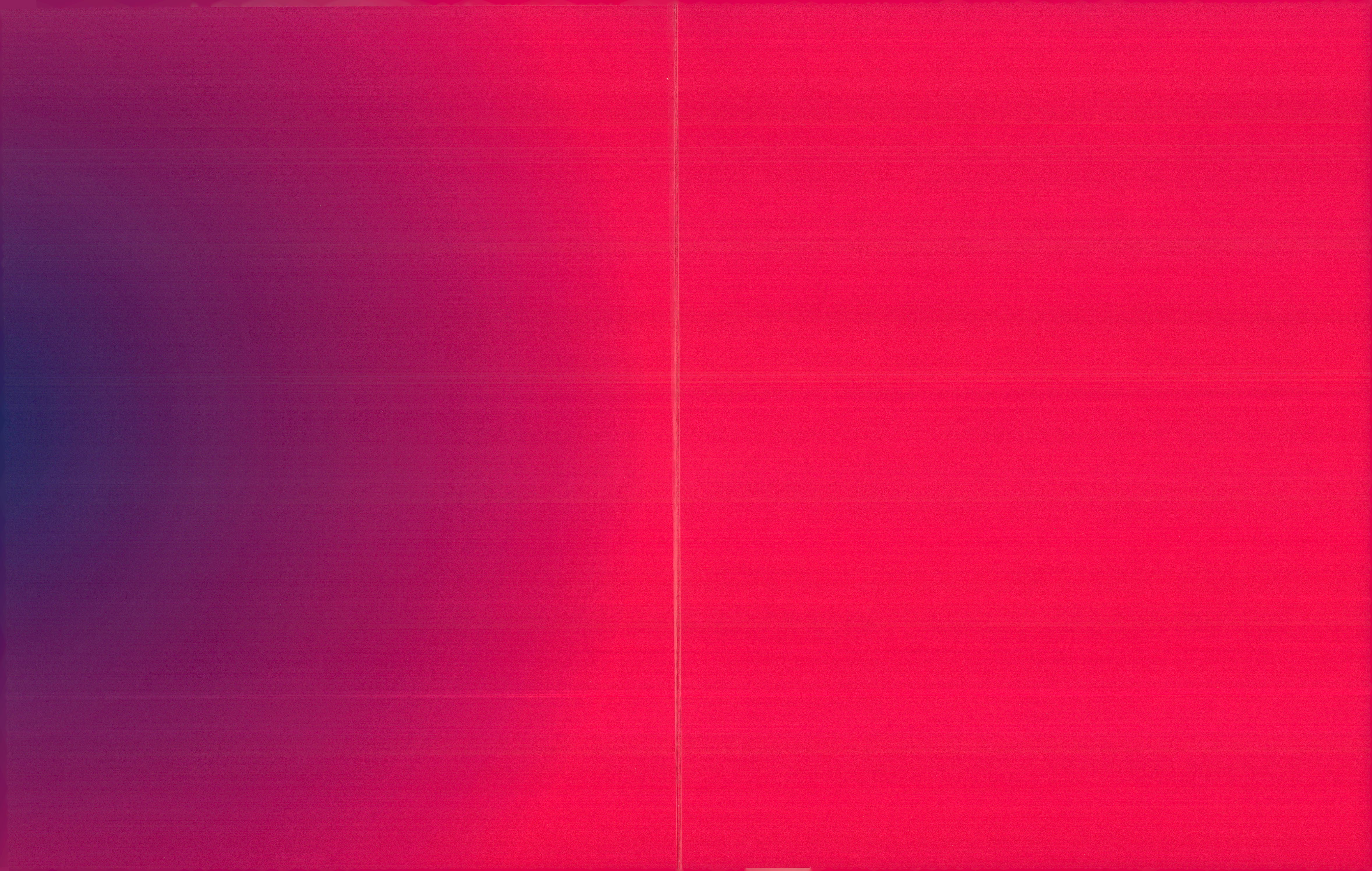

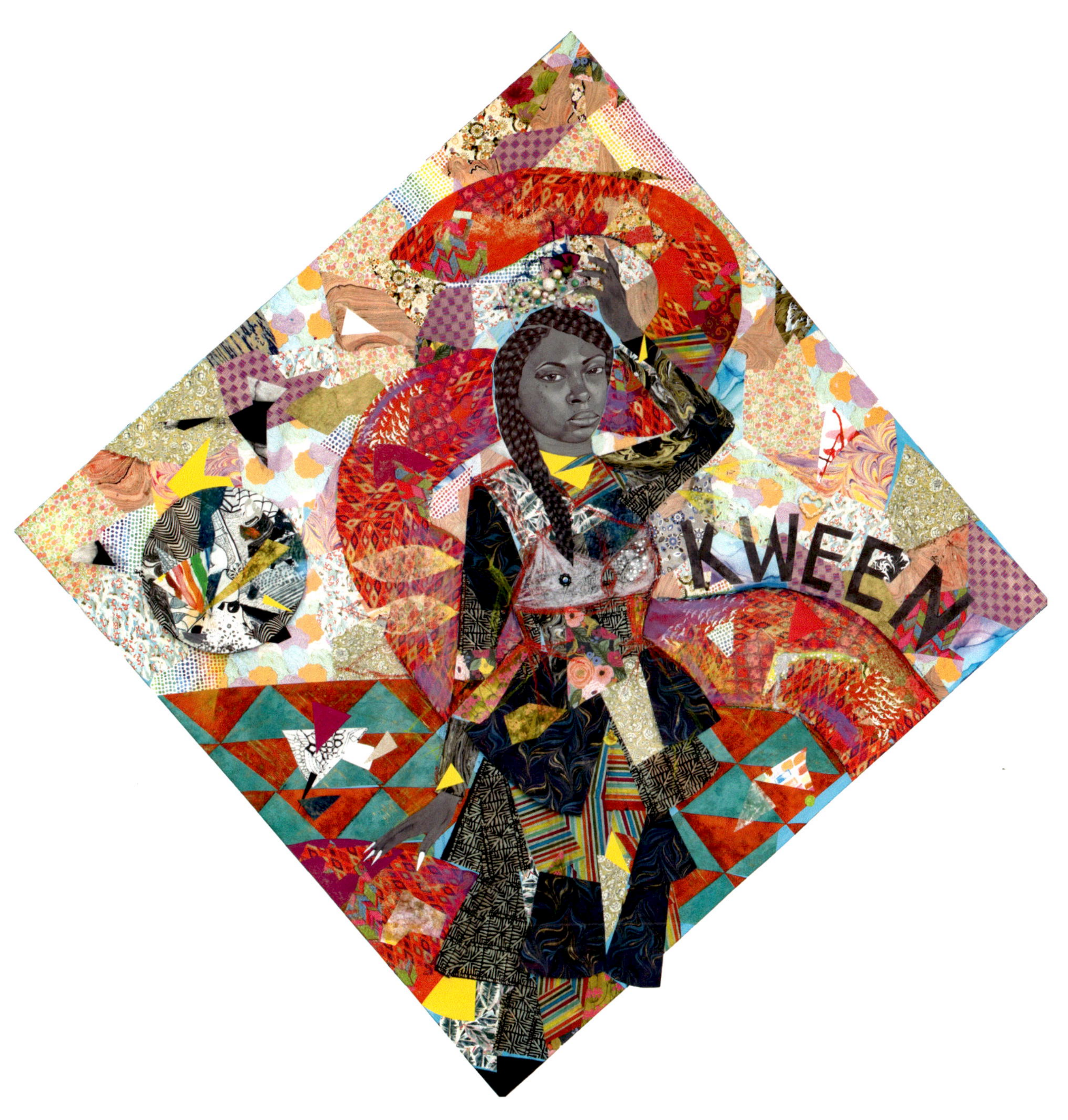

Prom Kween, 2019
Ink, acrylic, mixed media, colored pencil, fabric, glitter, and rhinestones on canvas
77 × 72 in.

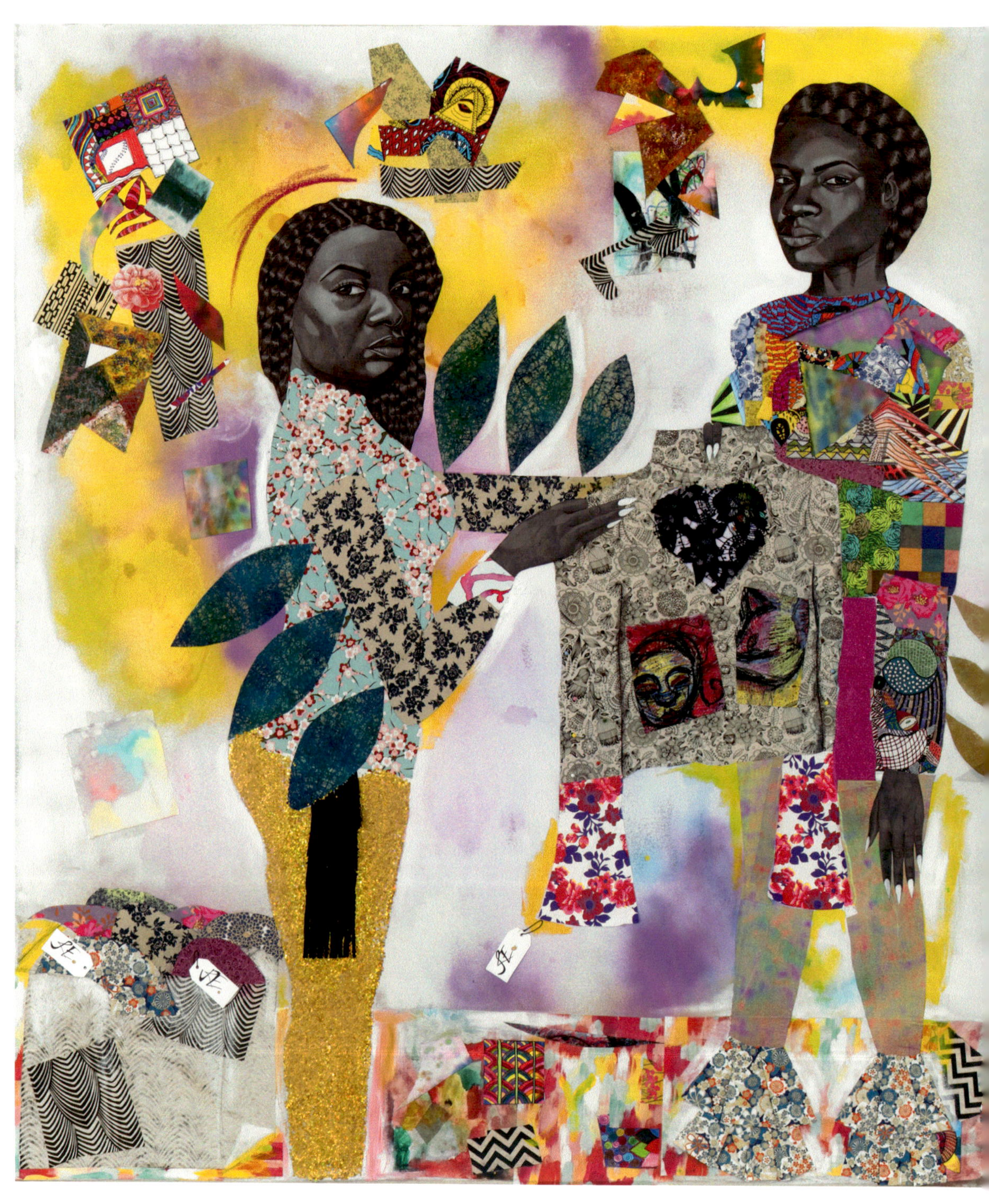

Shirt with Lace Heart (diptych), 2018
Acrylic, spray paint, glitter, ink, and collage on canvas
72 × 128 in. overall

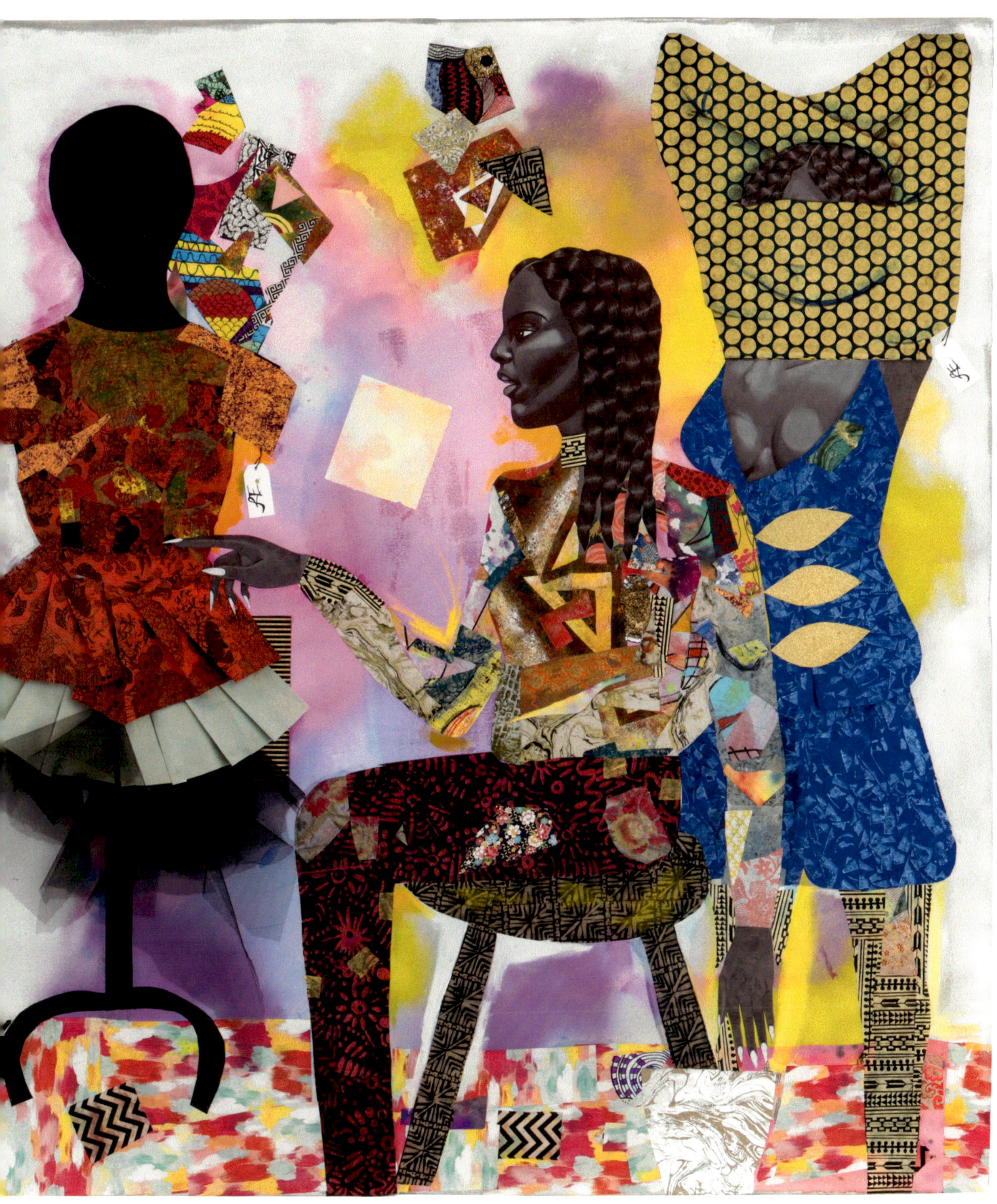

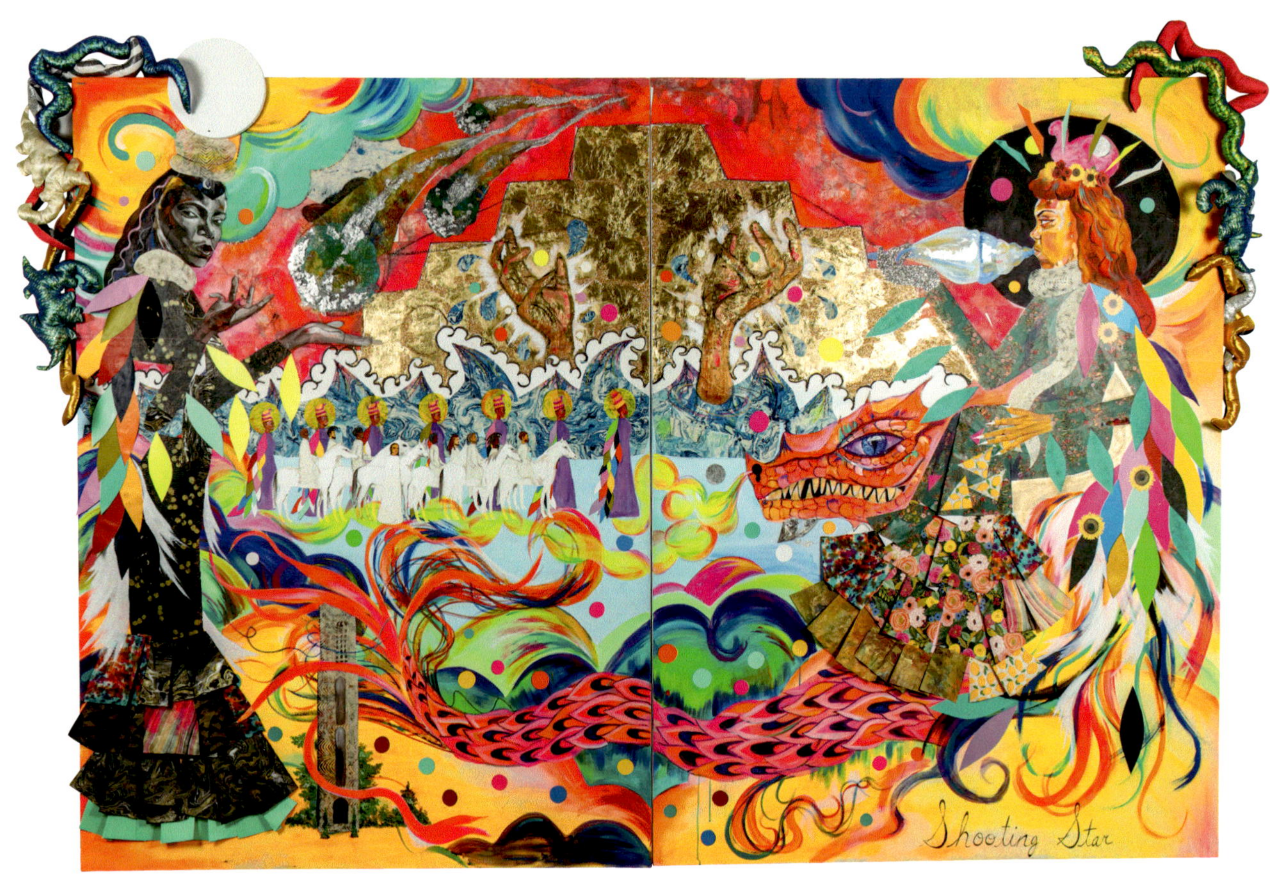

Lullaby for a Shooting Star (diptych), 2023
Acrylic, gold leaf, glitter, mixed-media collage,
and soft sculpture on canvas
96 × 144 in. overall

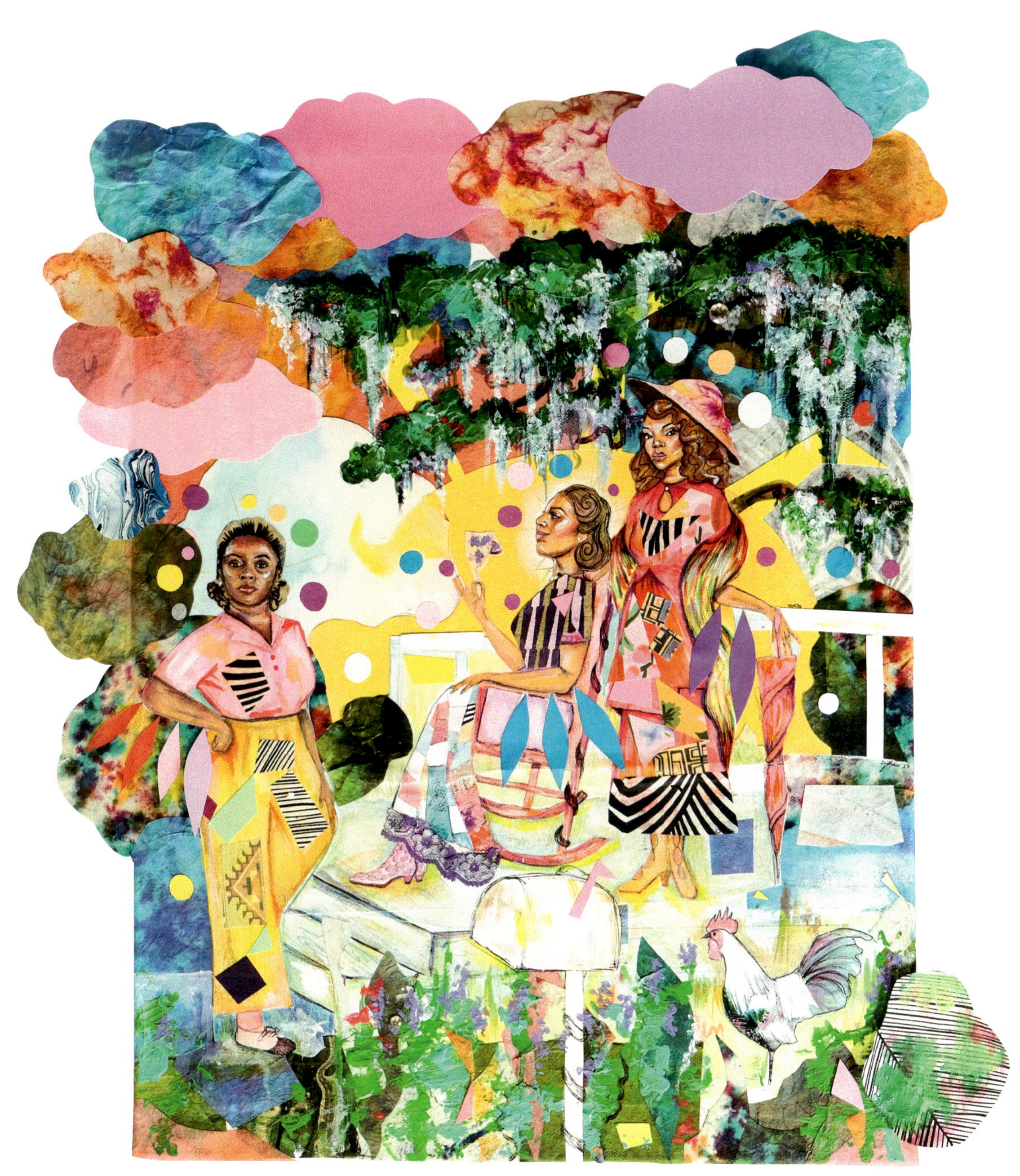

She Who Crowned Herself, 2022–23
Marker, colored pencil, and mixed-media collage on canvas
20 × 16 in.

THE UNRAVELING

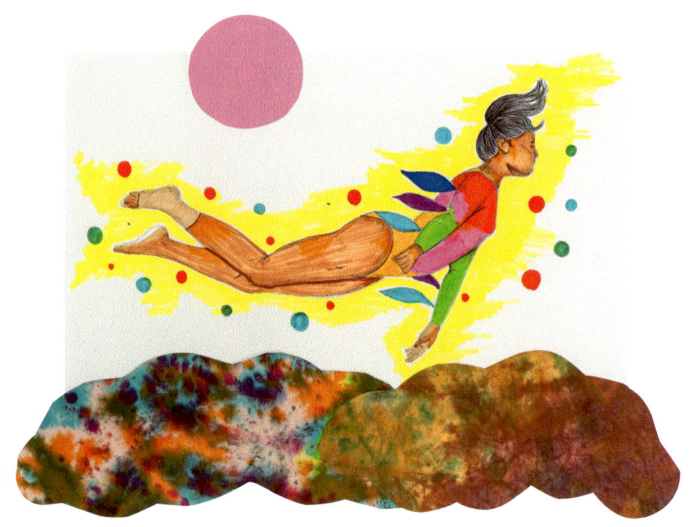

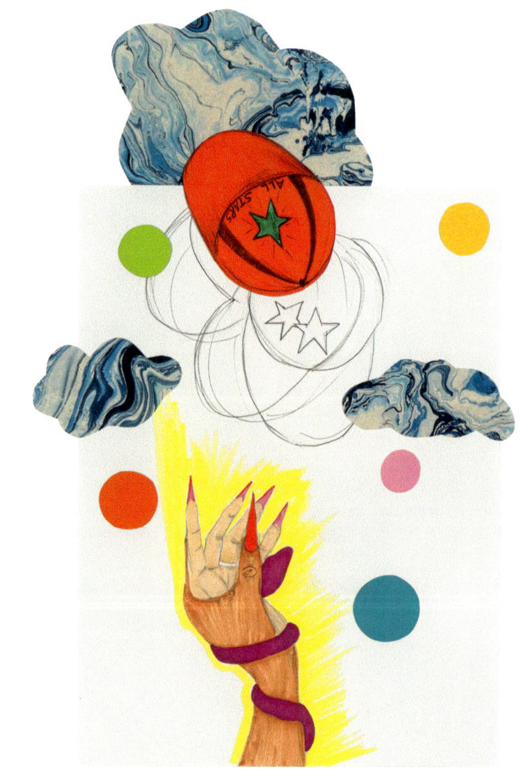

The Unraveling (suite of 12 drawings), 2023
Marker, colored pencil, and mixed-media collage on paper
9 × 12 in. each, unframed

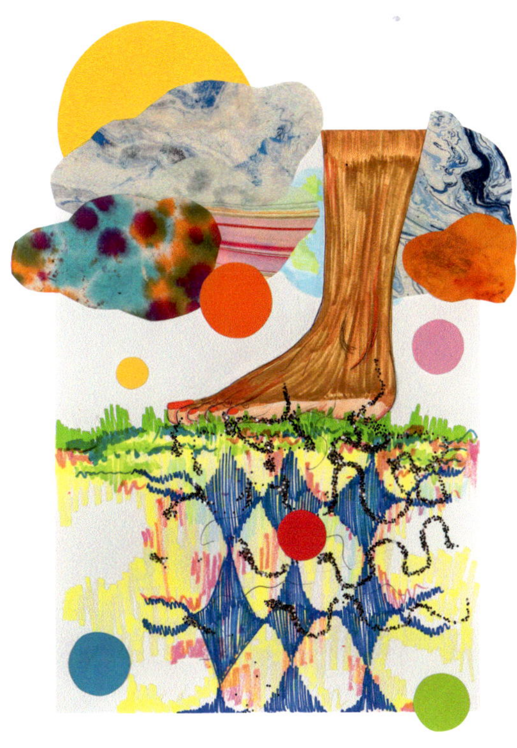

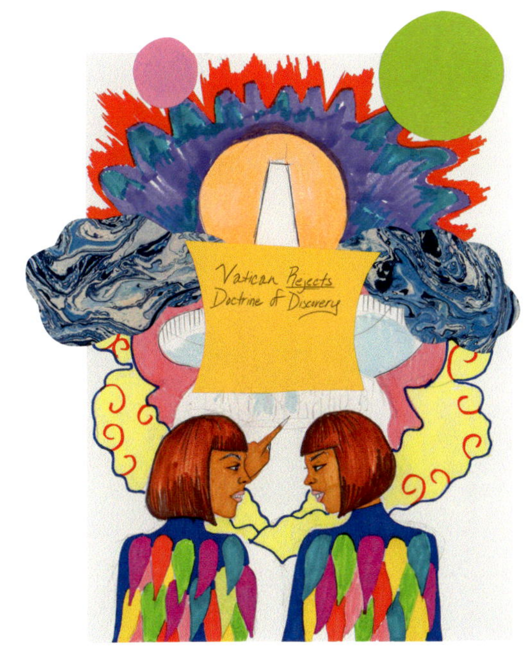
Vatican Rejects
Doctrine of Discovery

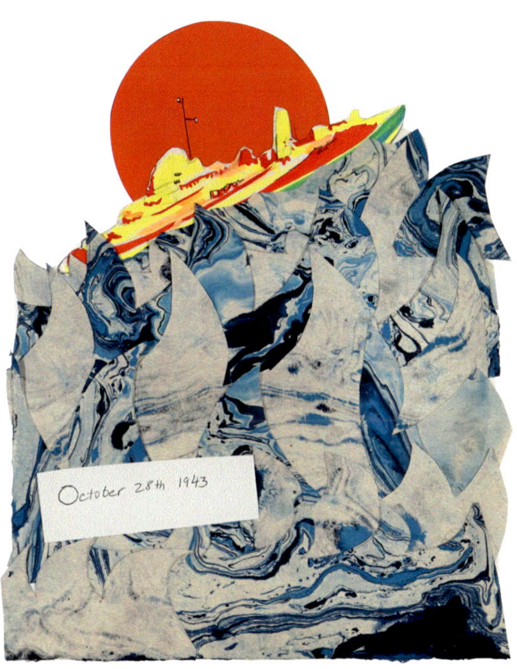
October 28th 1943

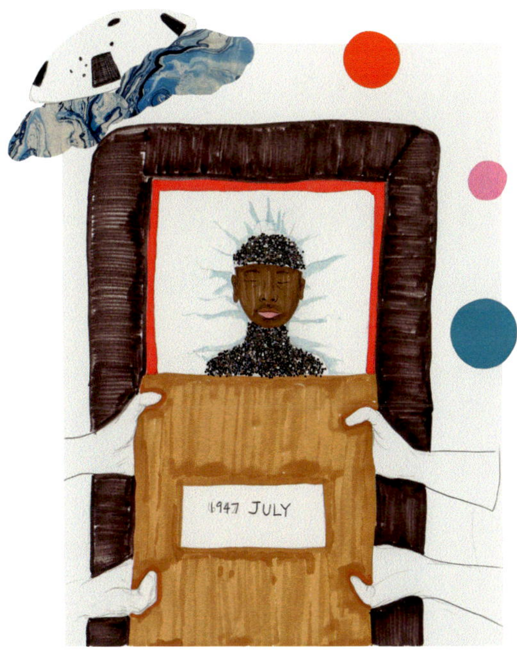
1947 JULY

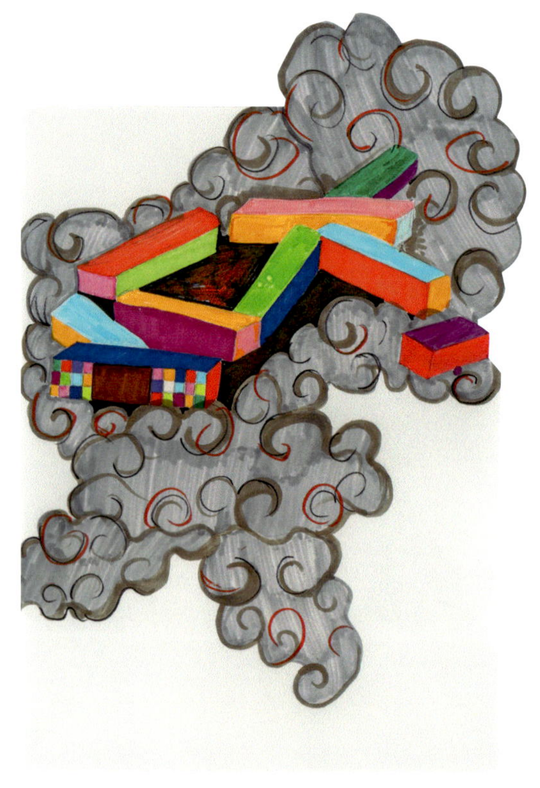

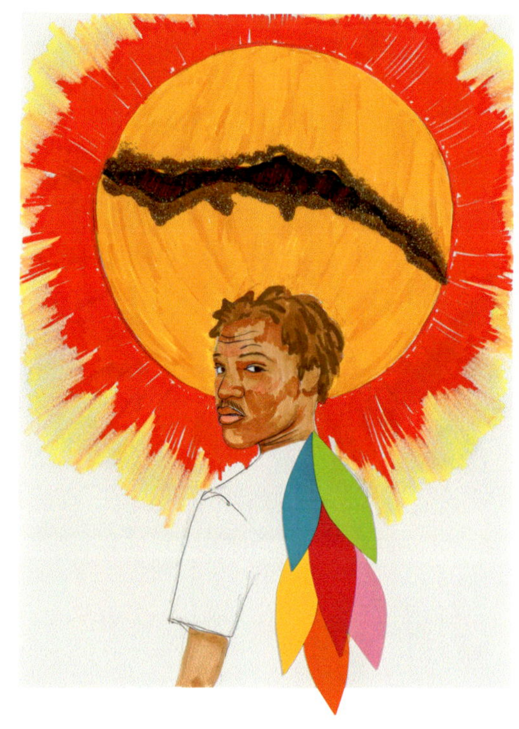

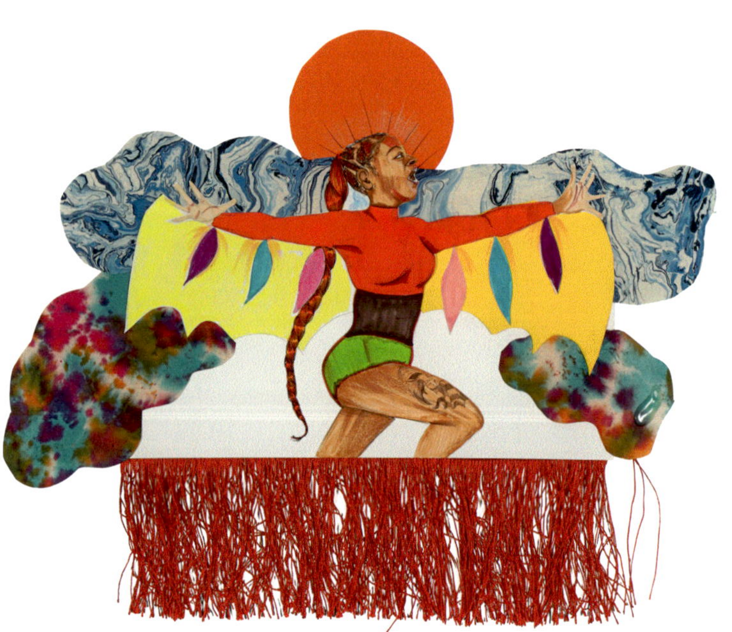

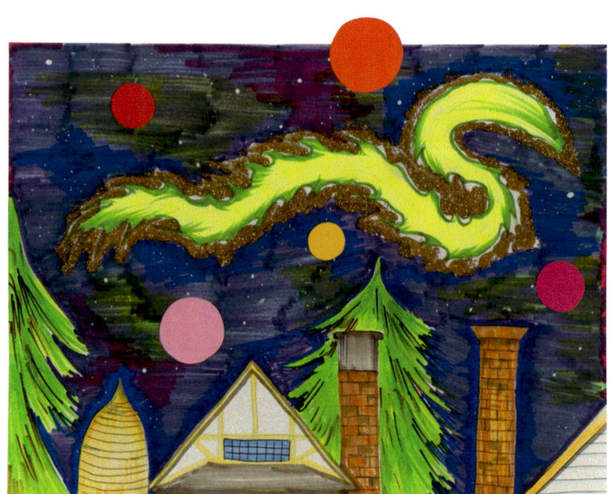

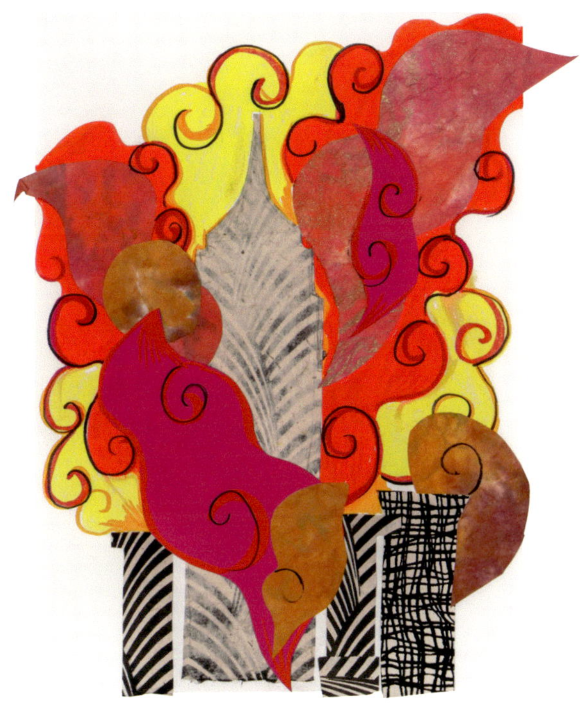

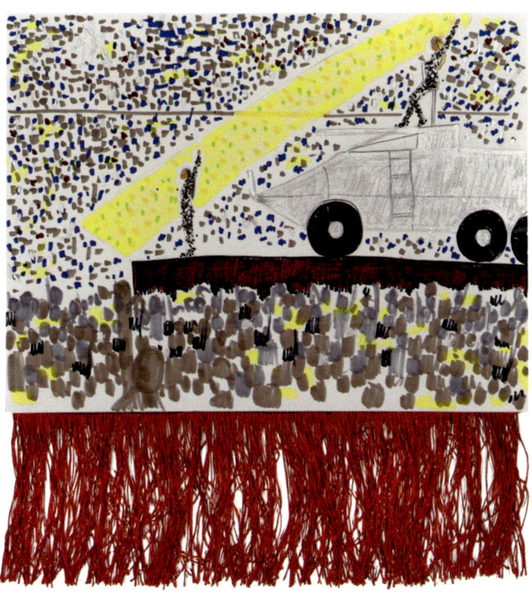

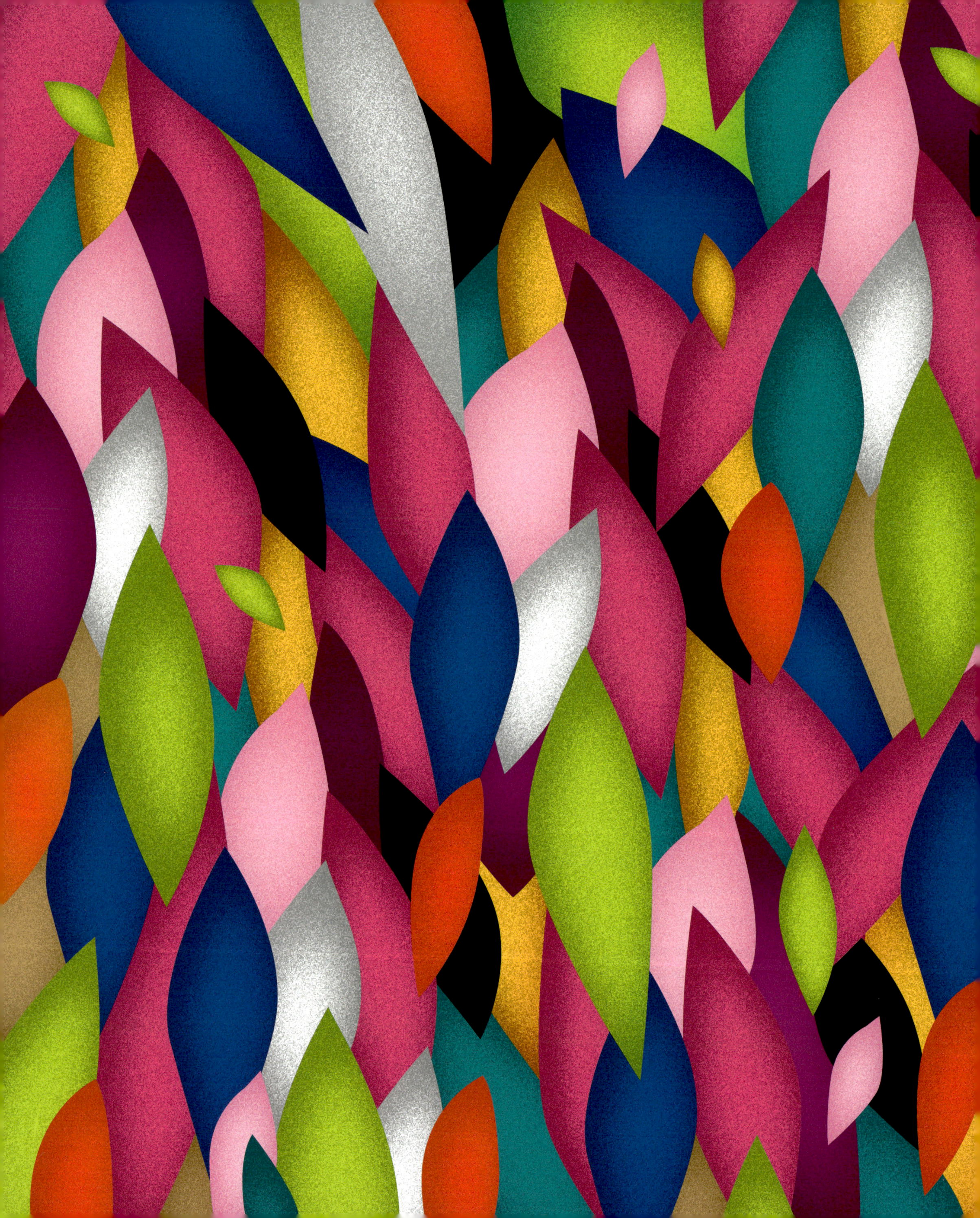

ANCIENT FUTURE

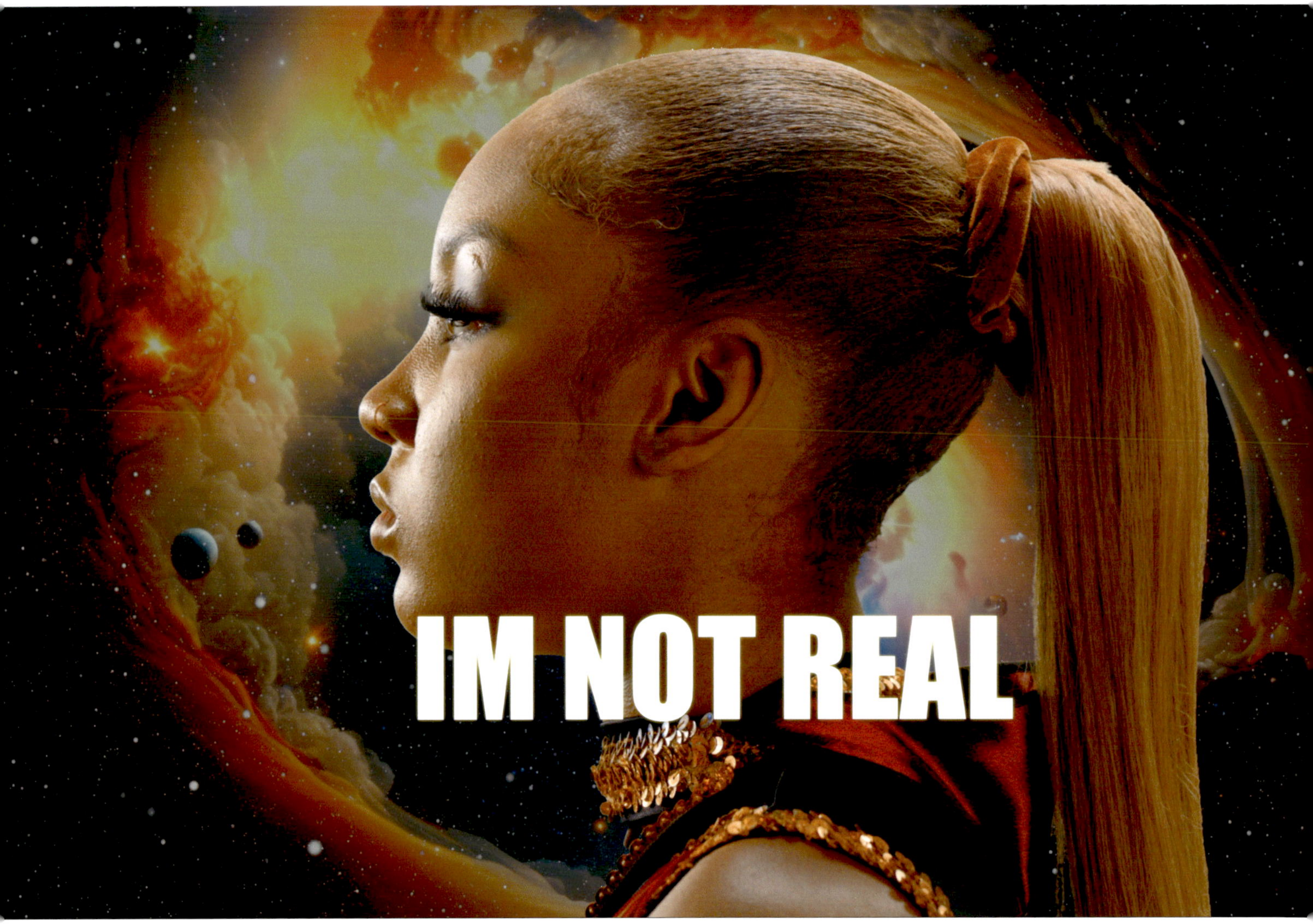

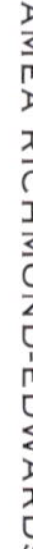

Ancient Future, 2023
Digital film, color, sound; 7 minutes

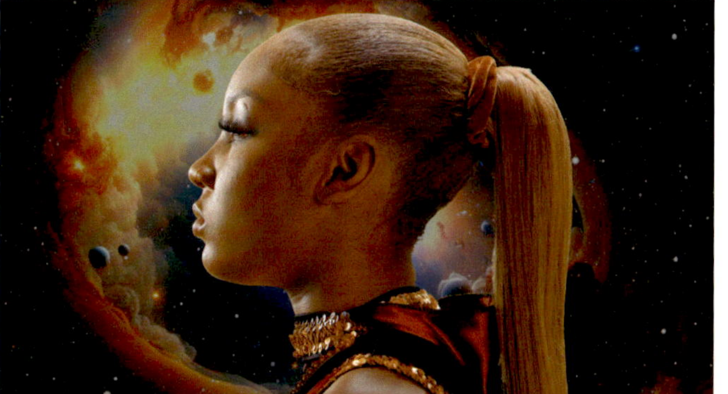

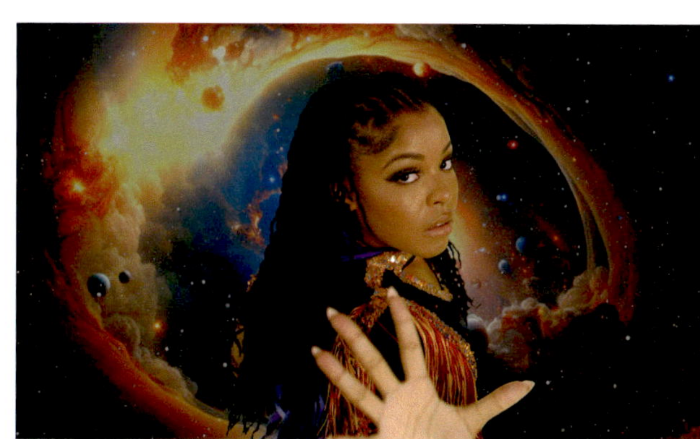

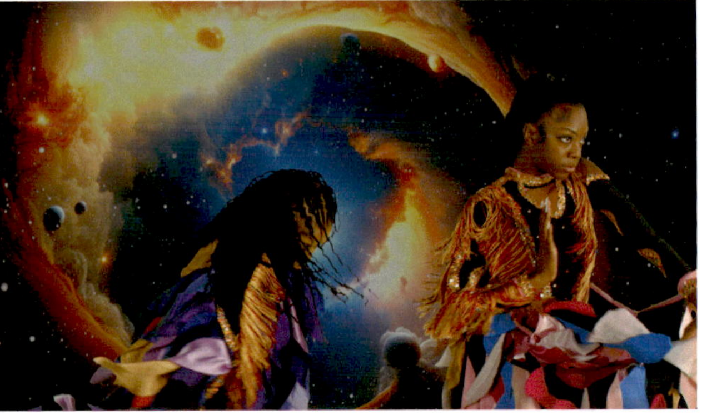

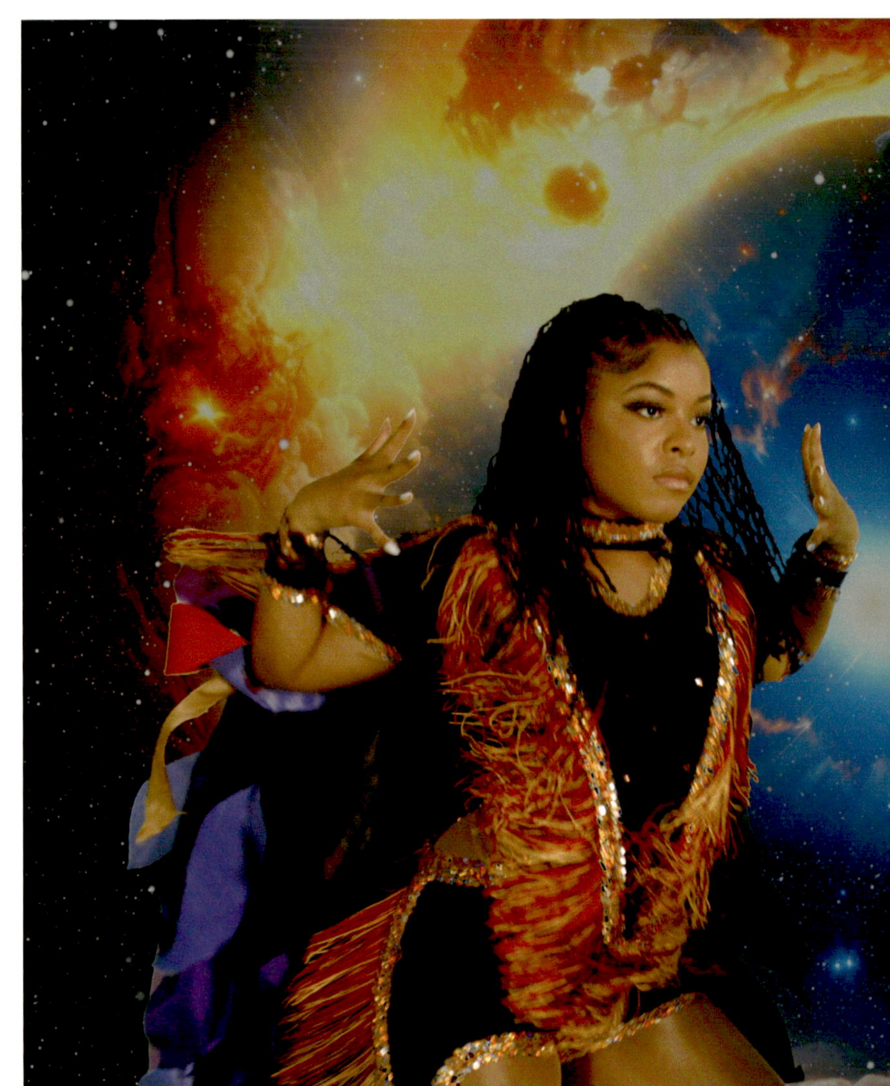

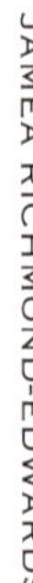
JAMEA RICHMOND-EDWARDS

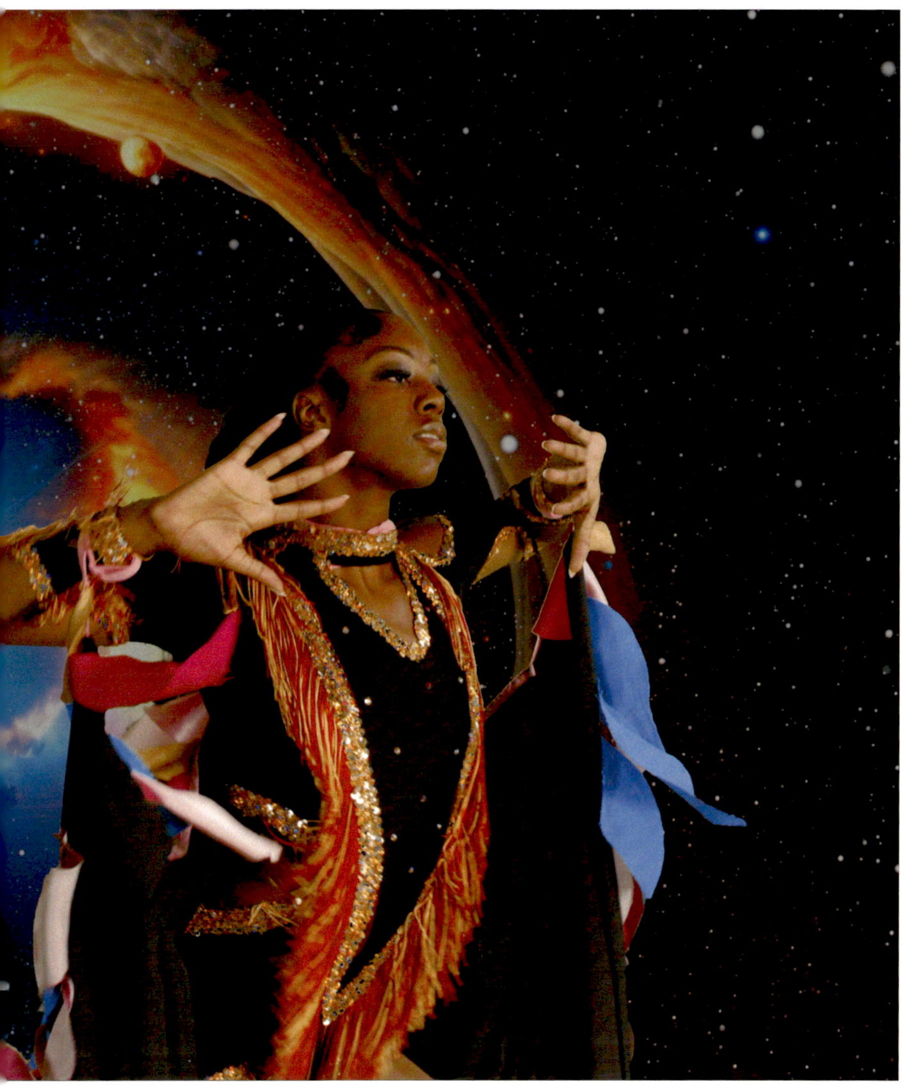

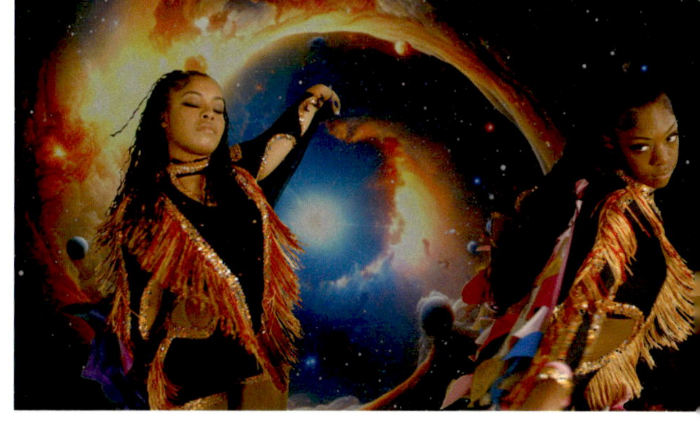

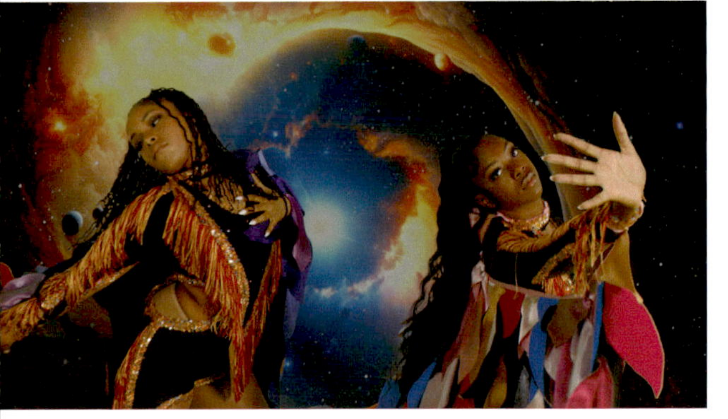

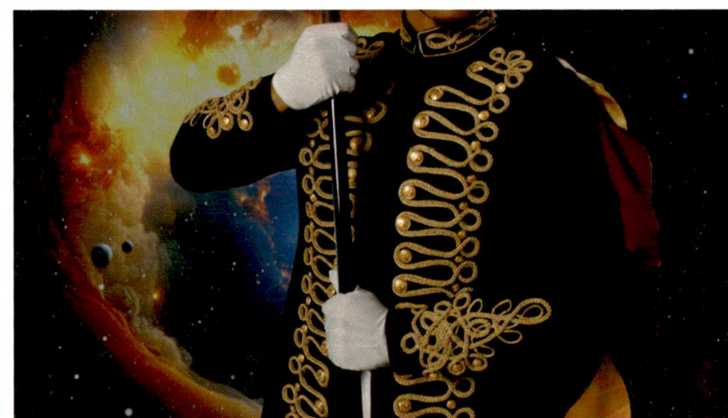

JAMEA RICHMOND-EDWARDS

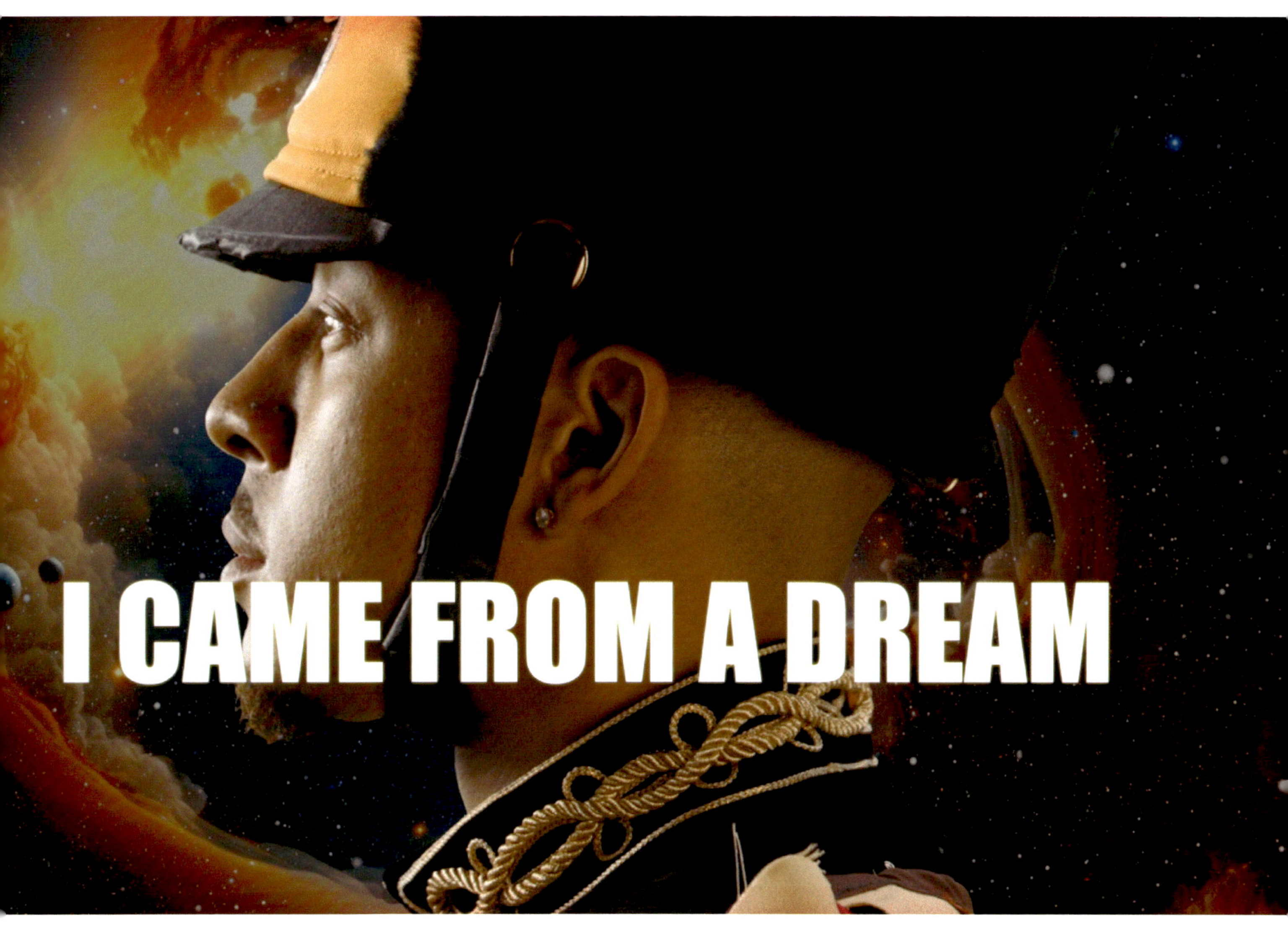
I CAME FROM A DREAM

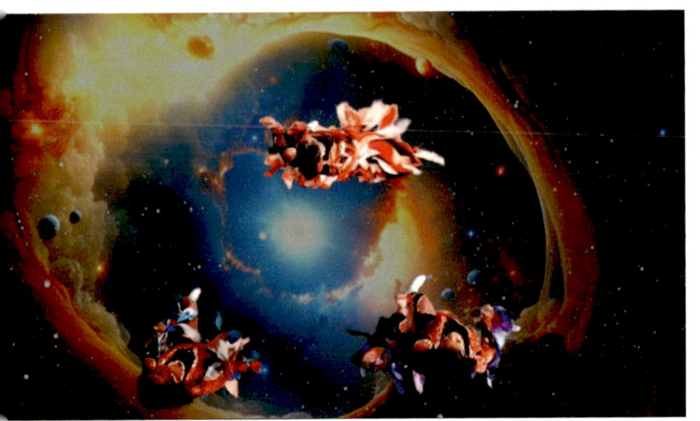

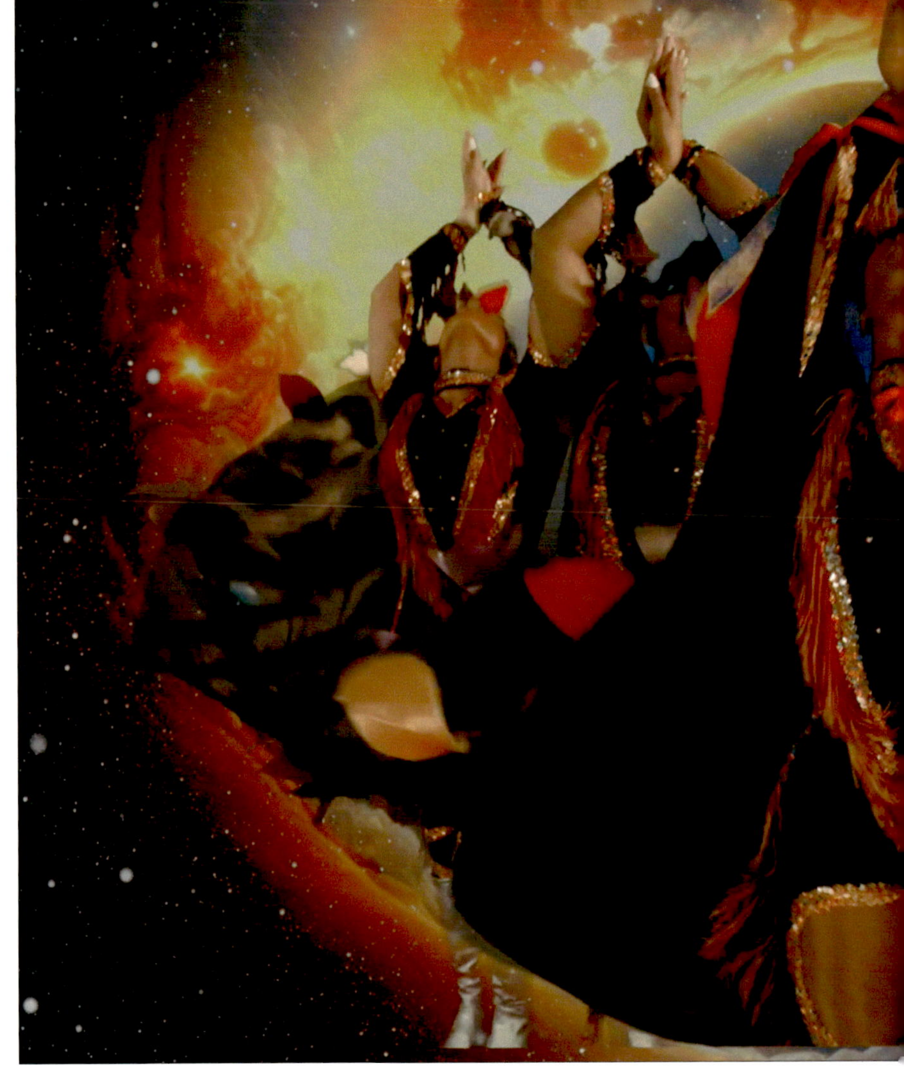

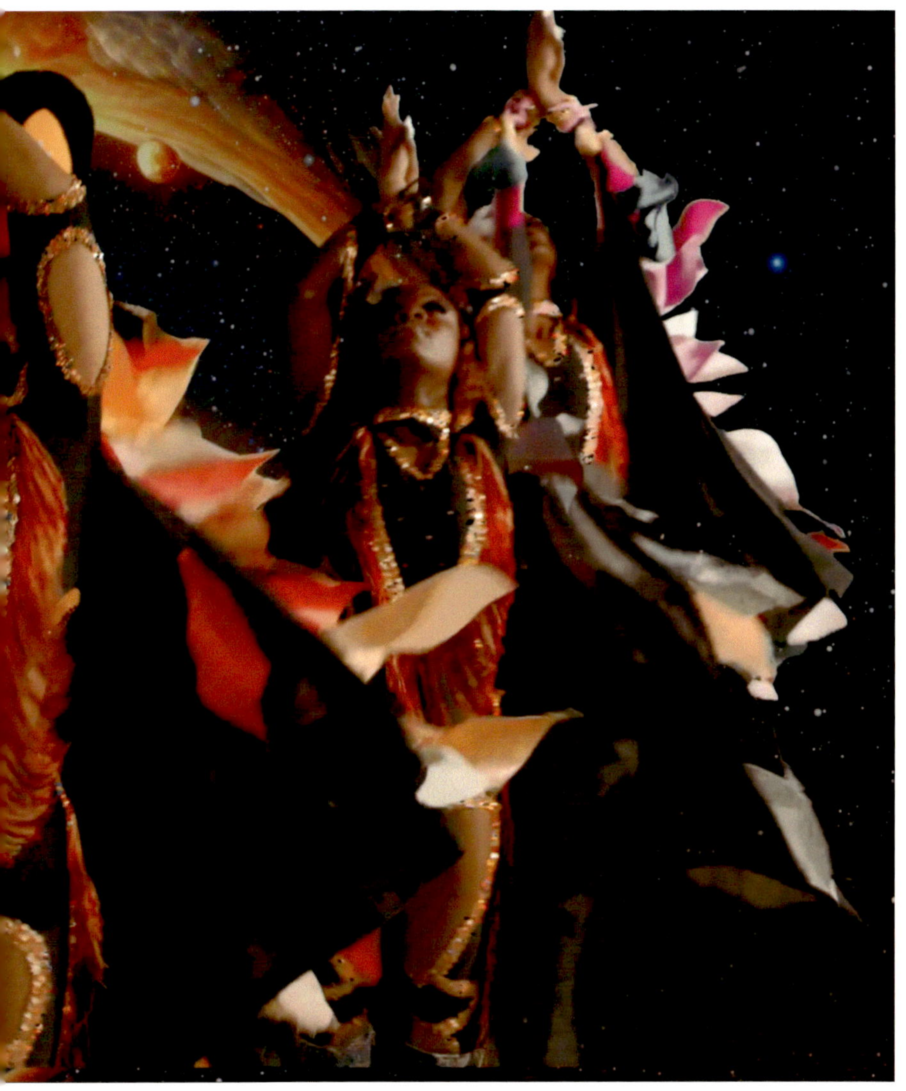

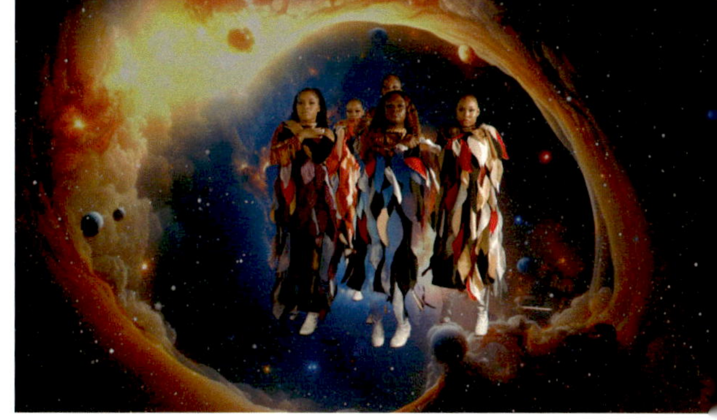

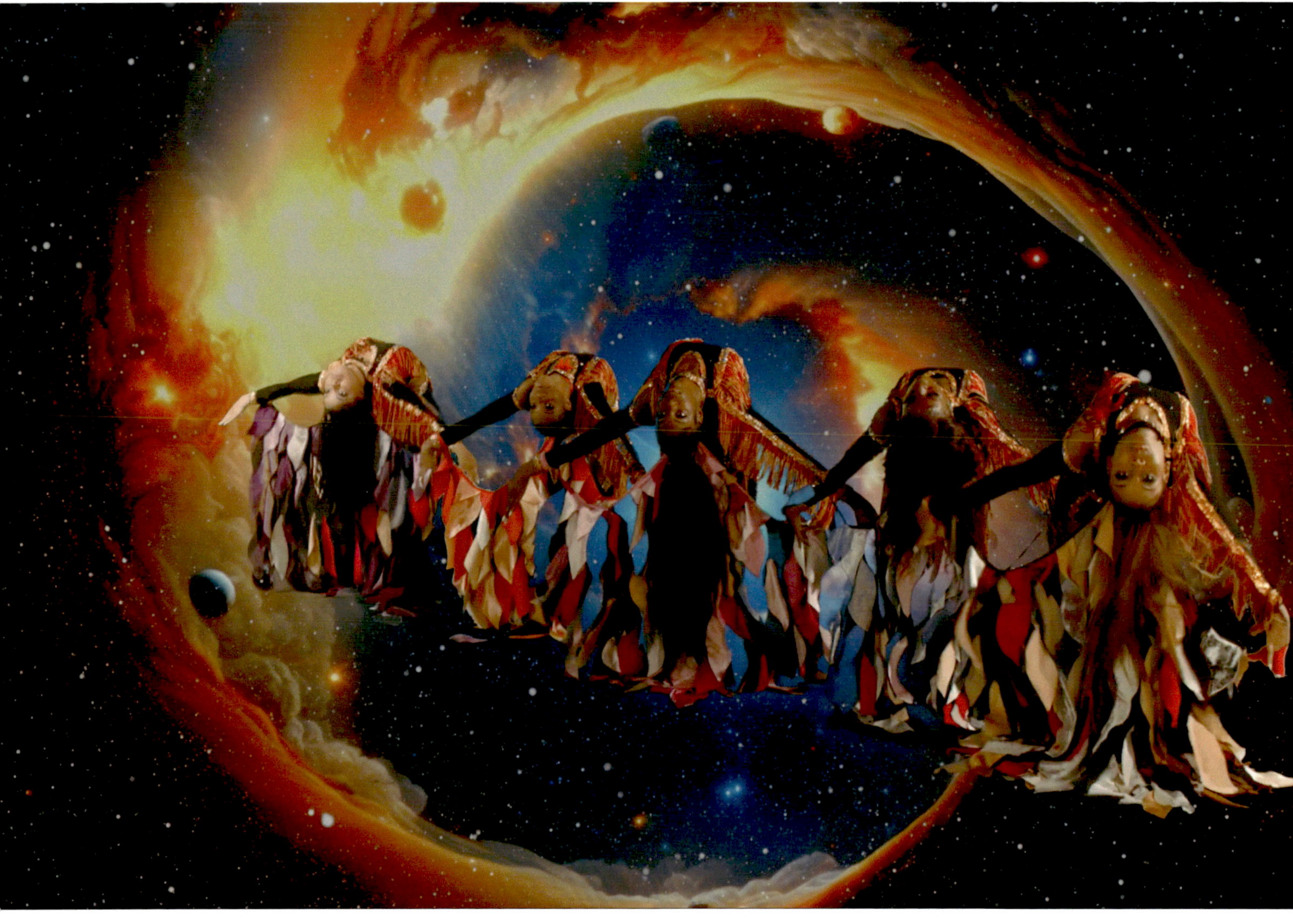

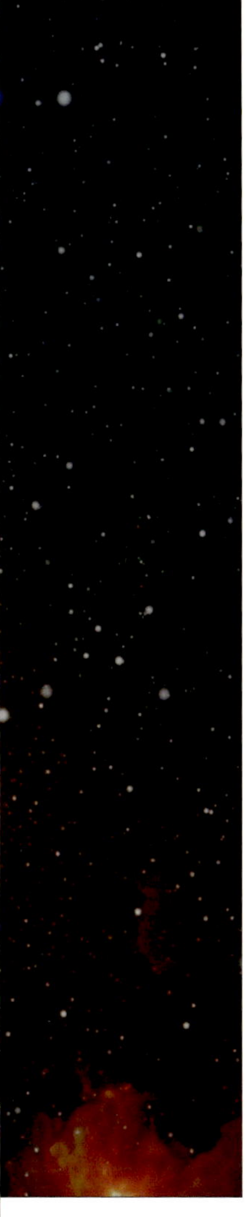

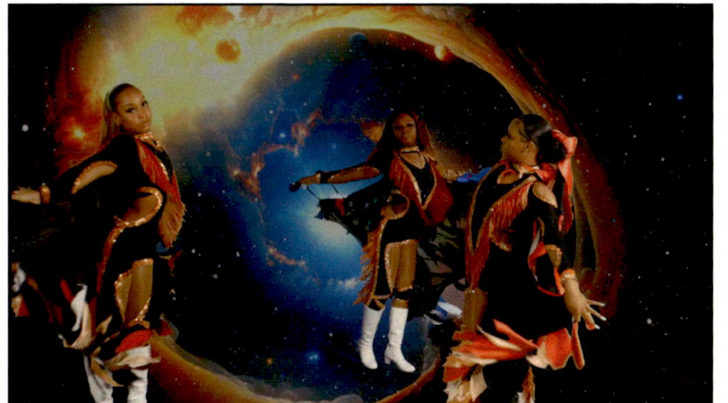

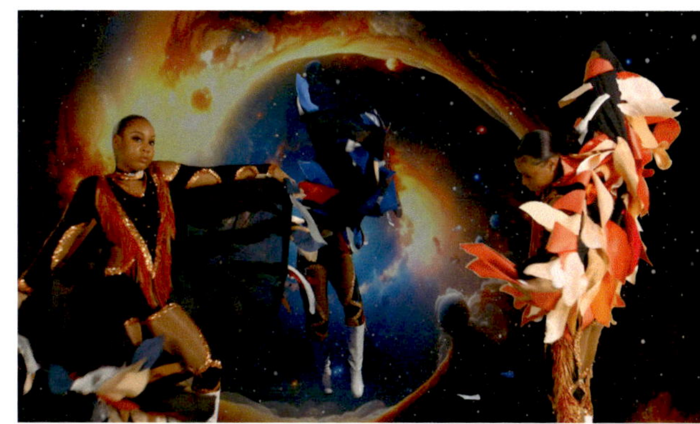

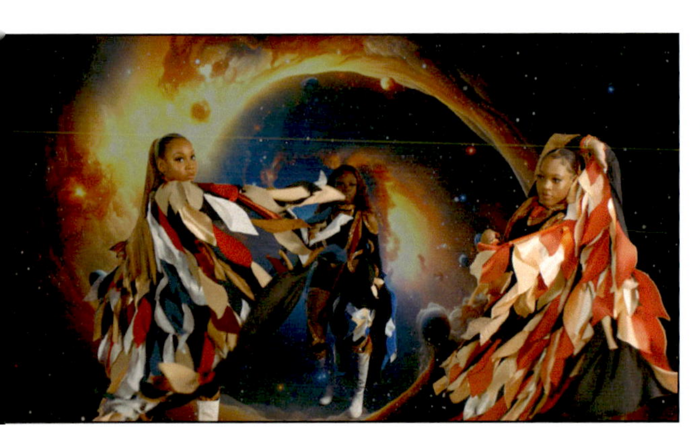

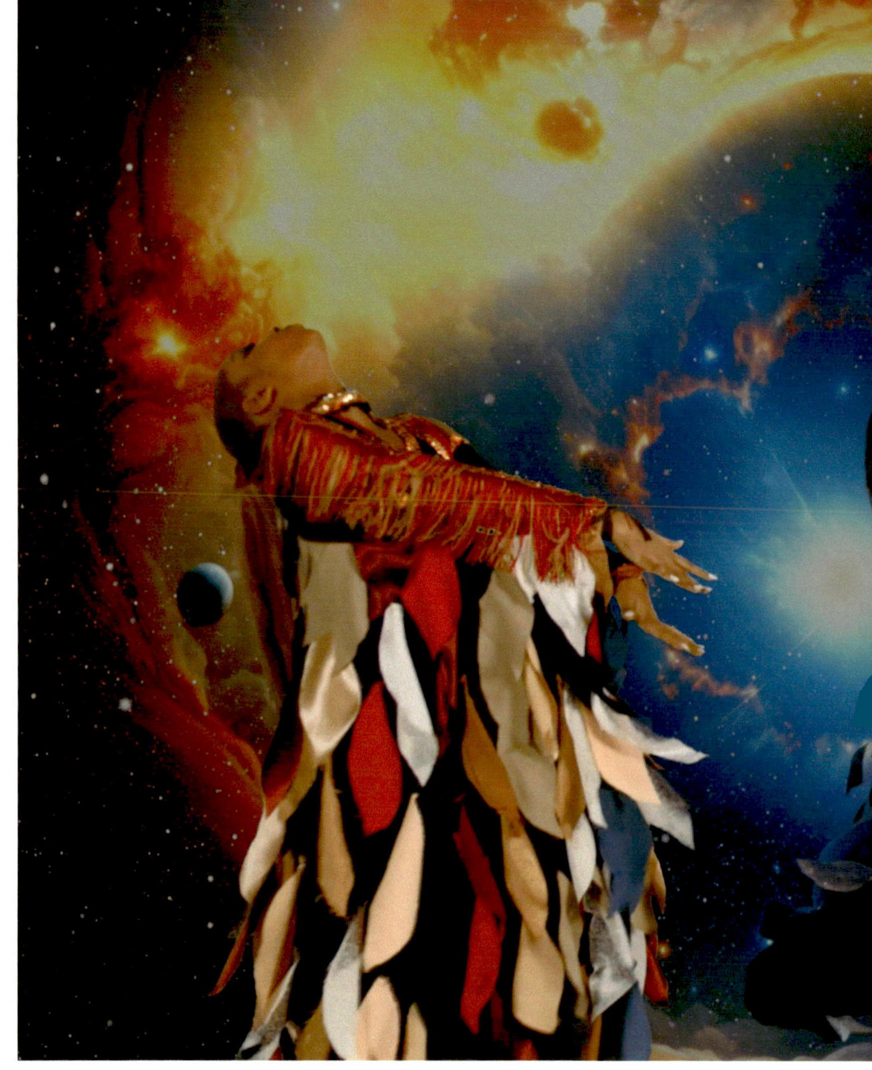

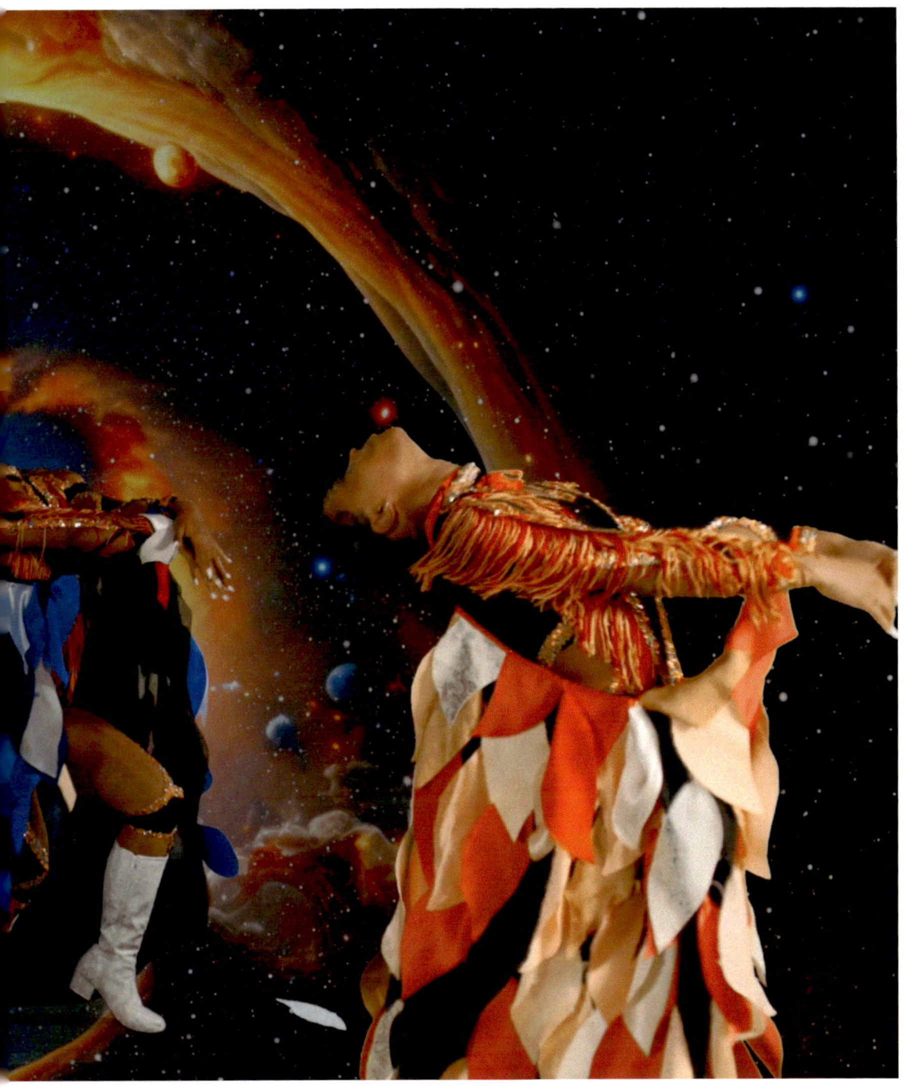

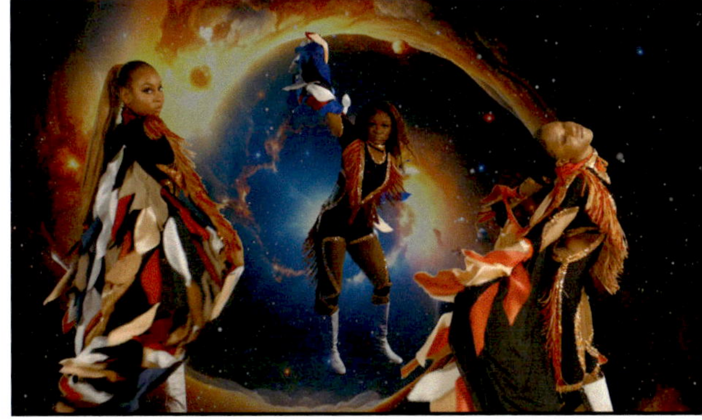

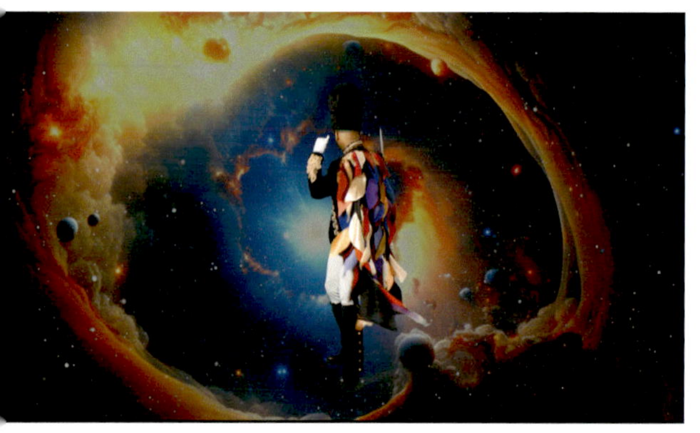

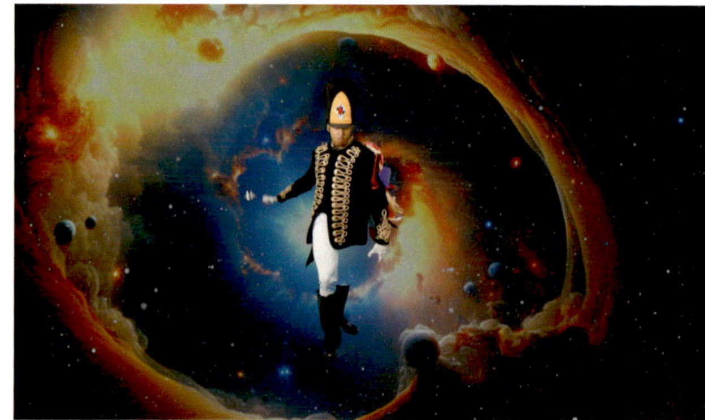

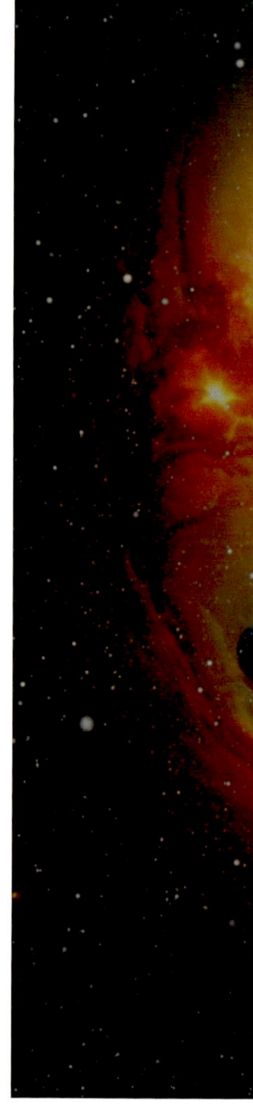

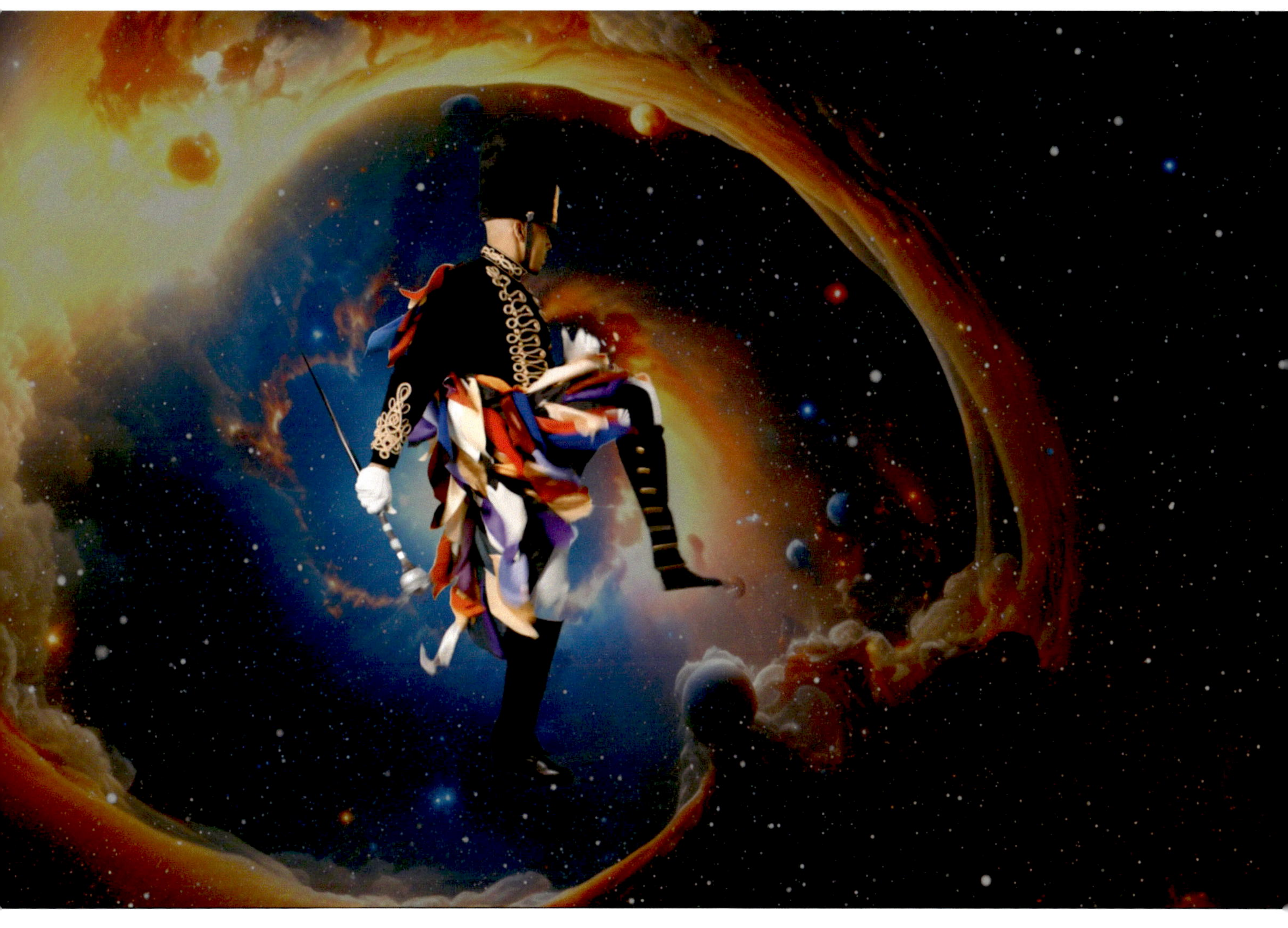

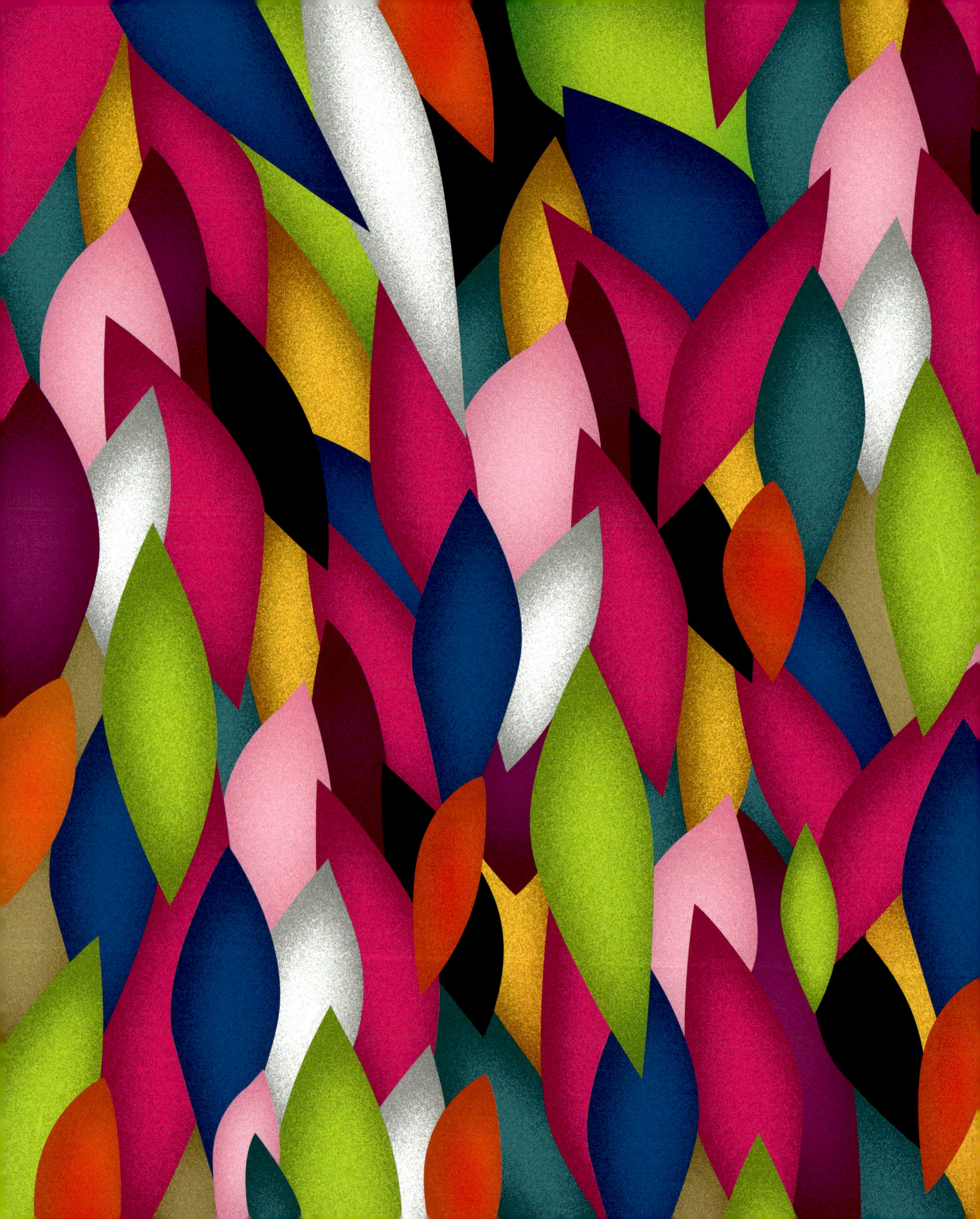

INSTALLATION VIEWS

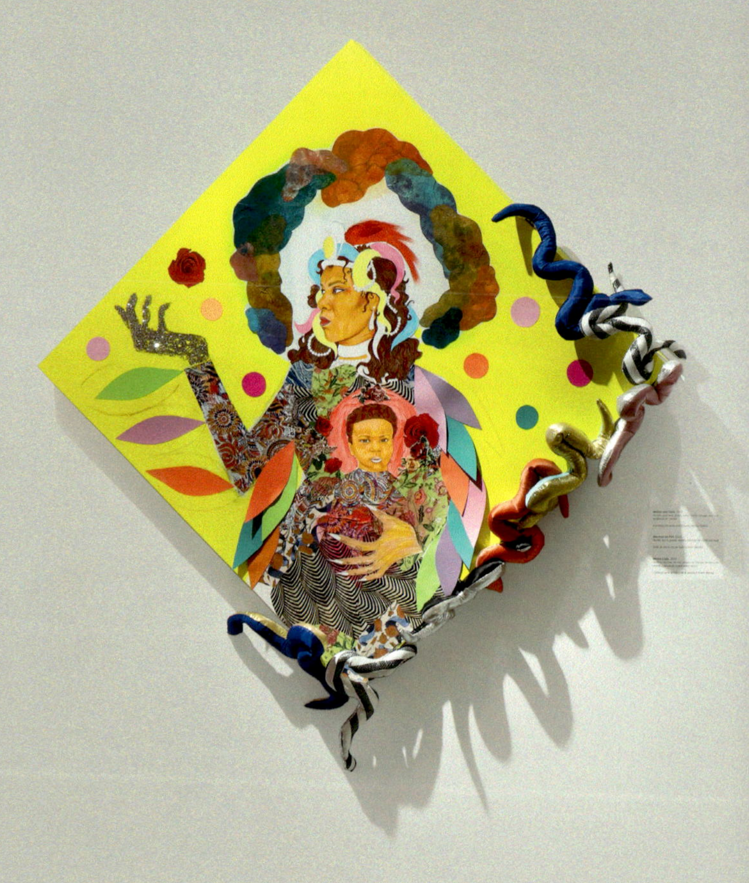
Richard Shack Gallery

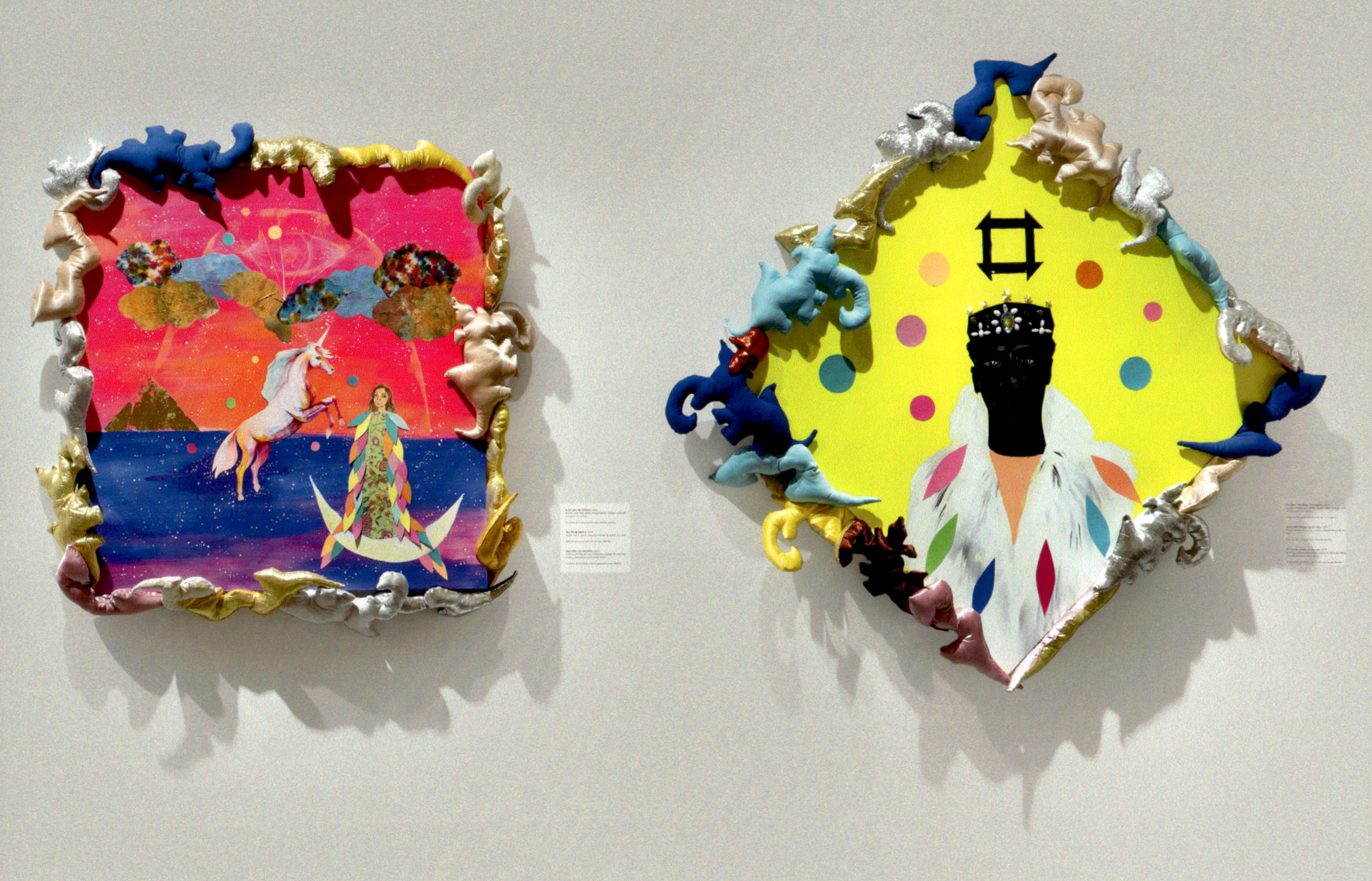

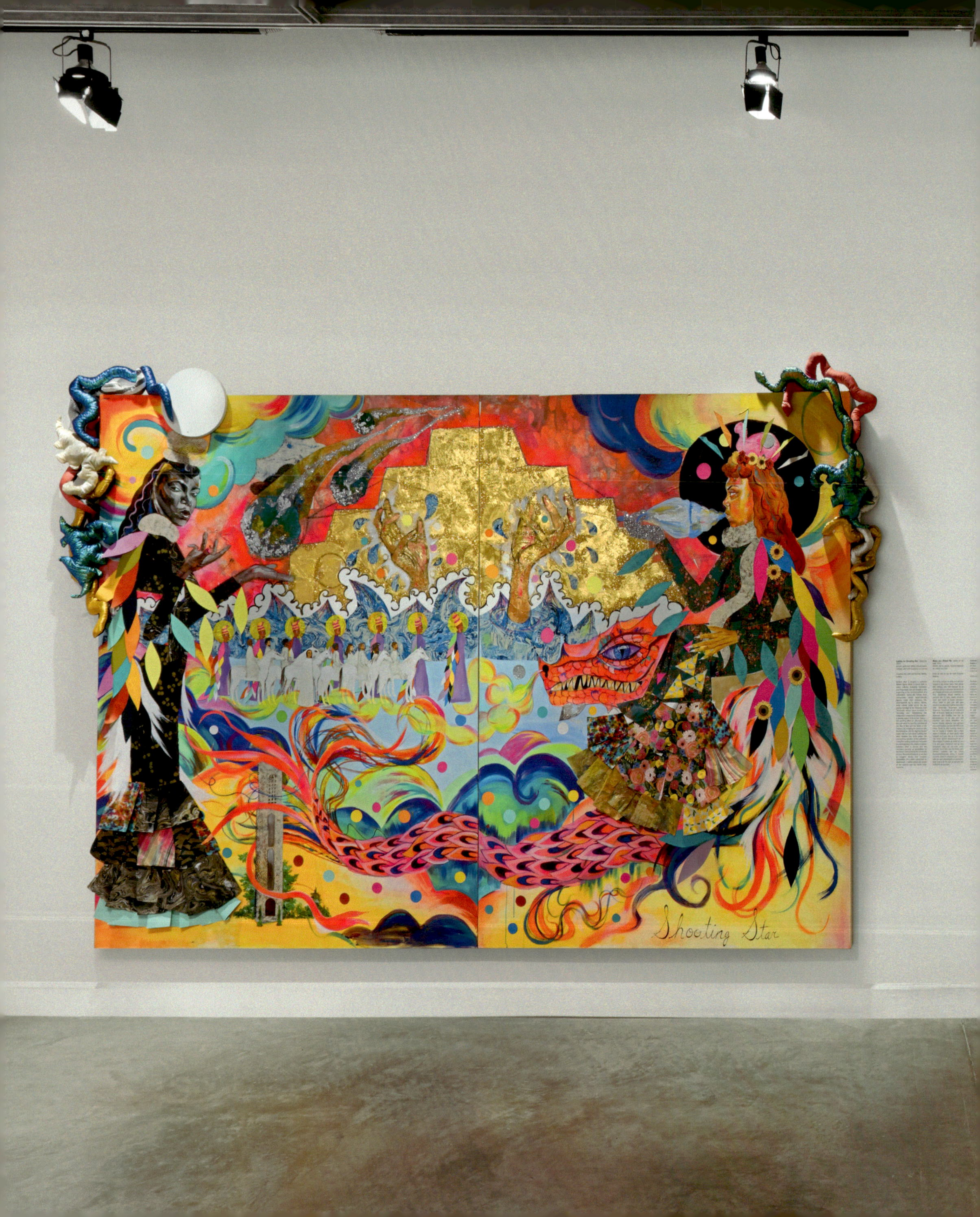

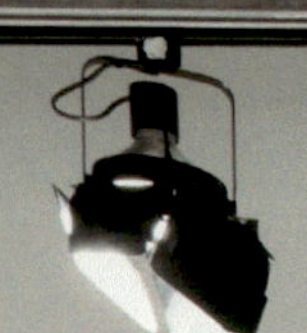

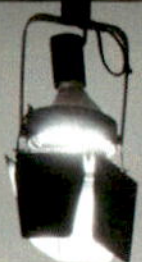

Shooting Star

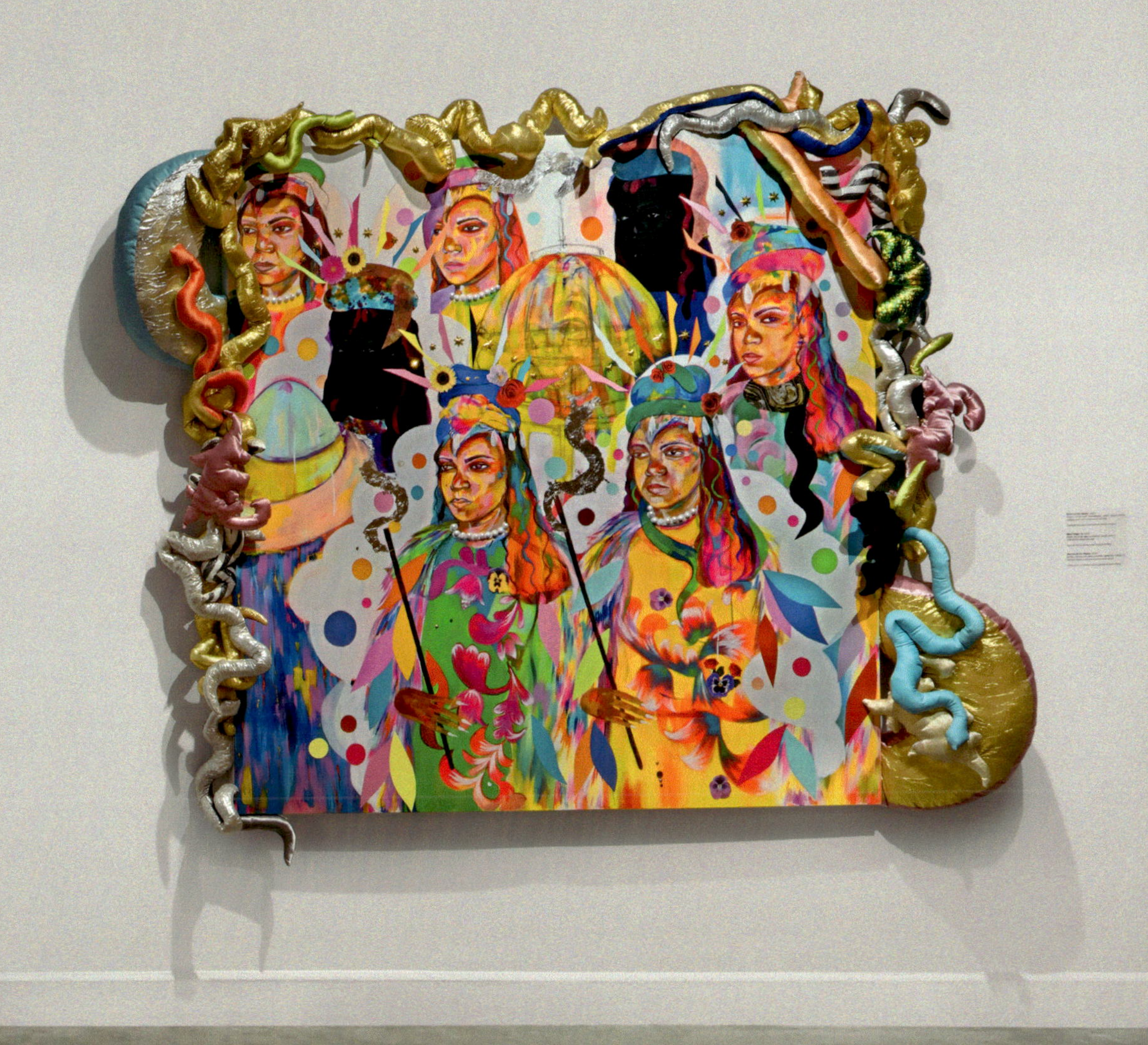

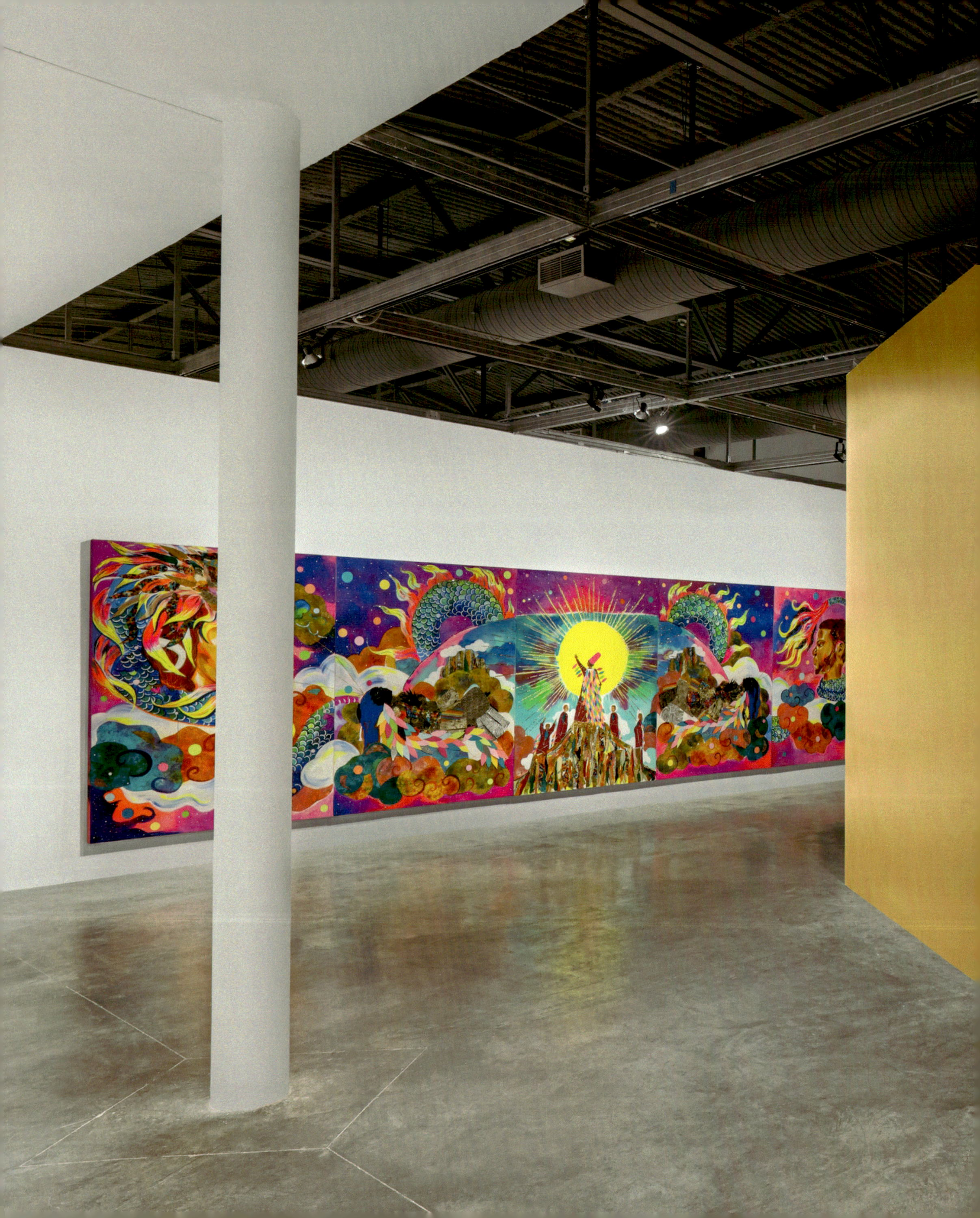

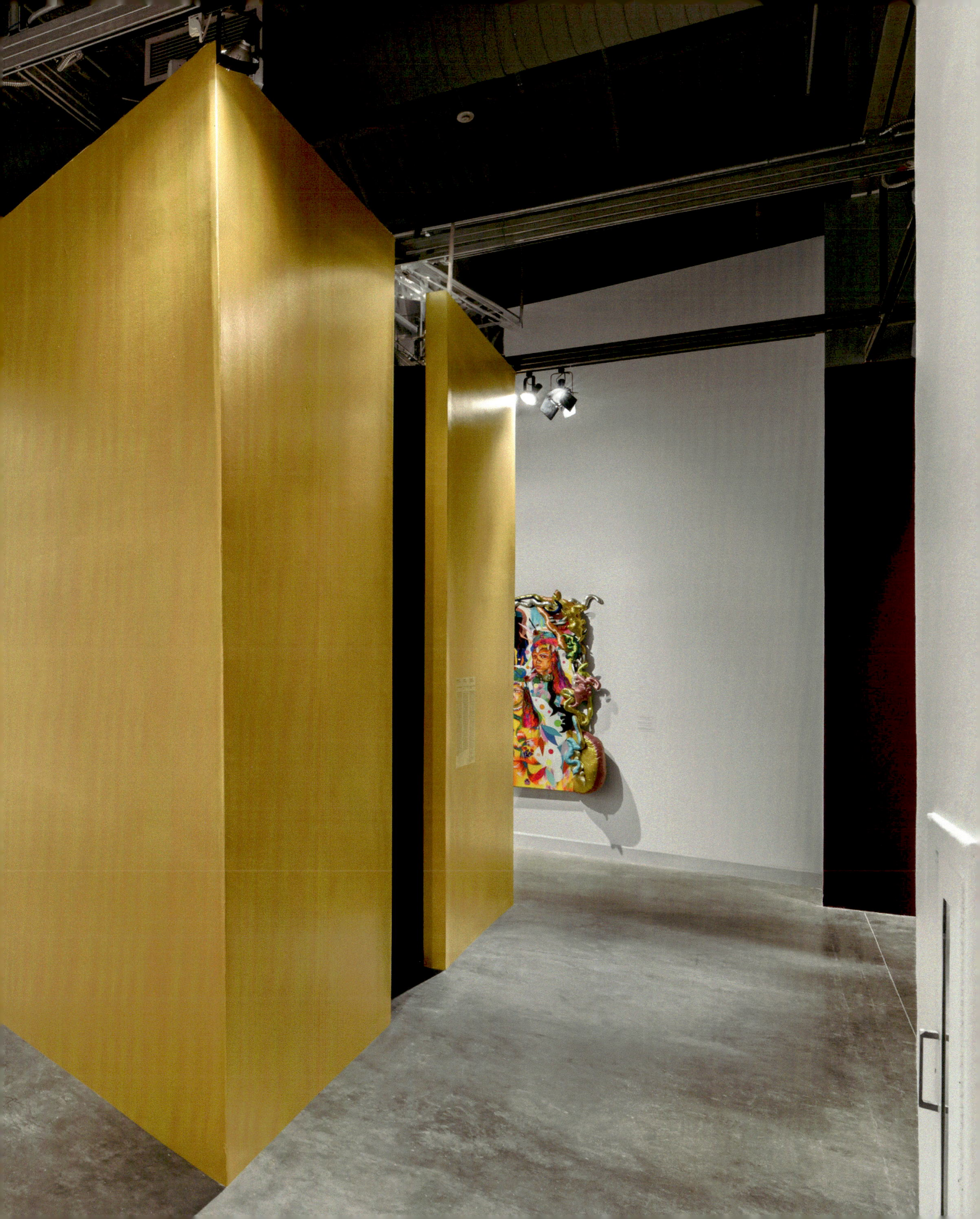

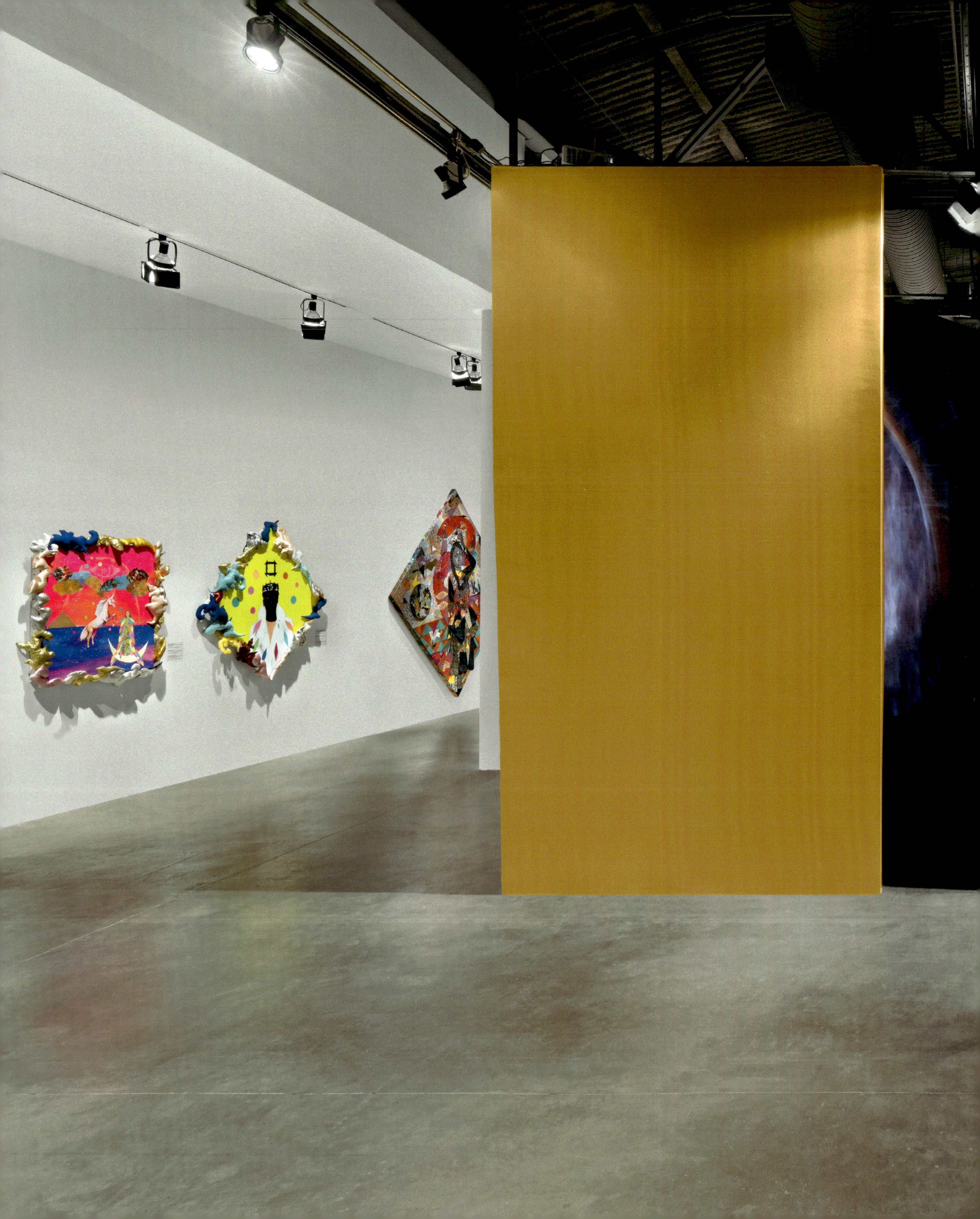

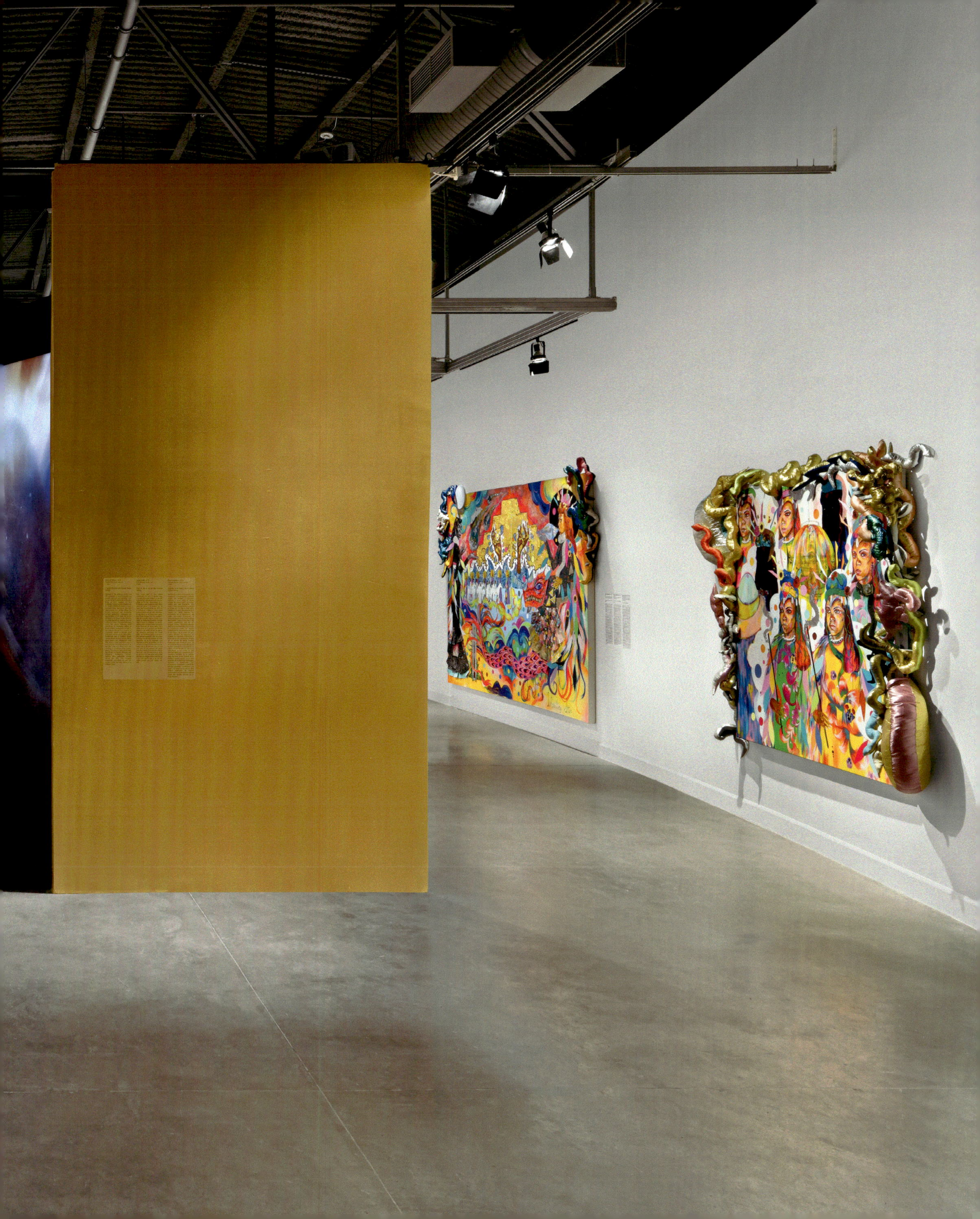

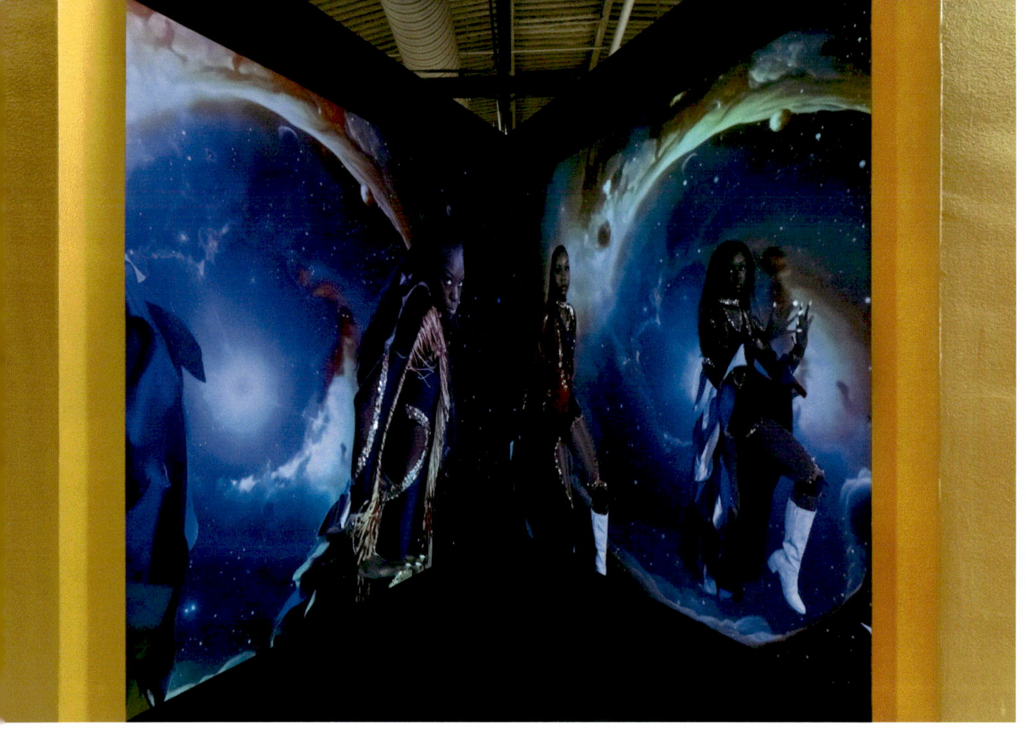

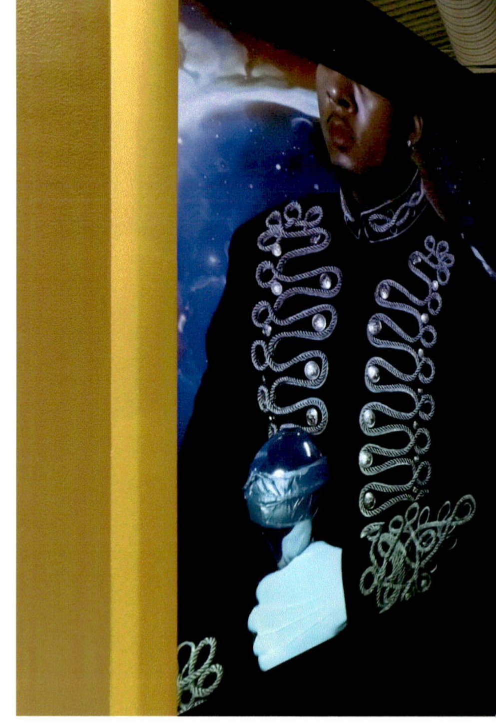

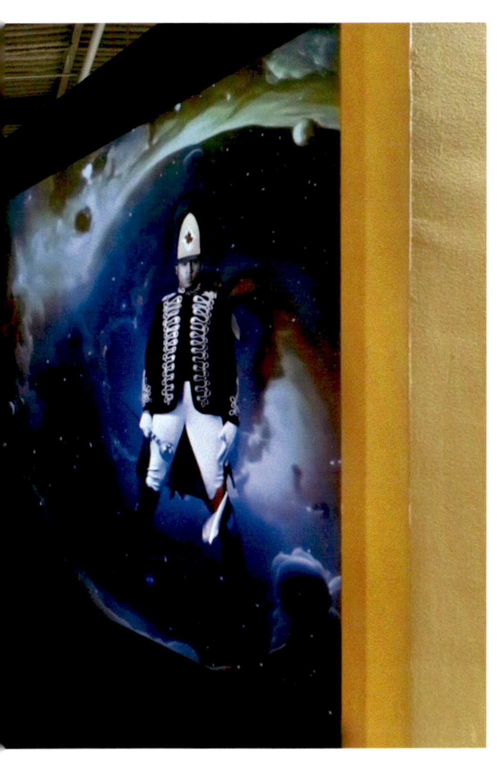

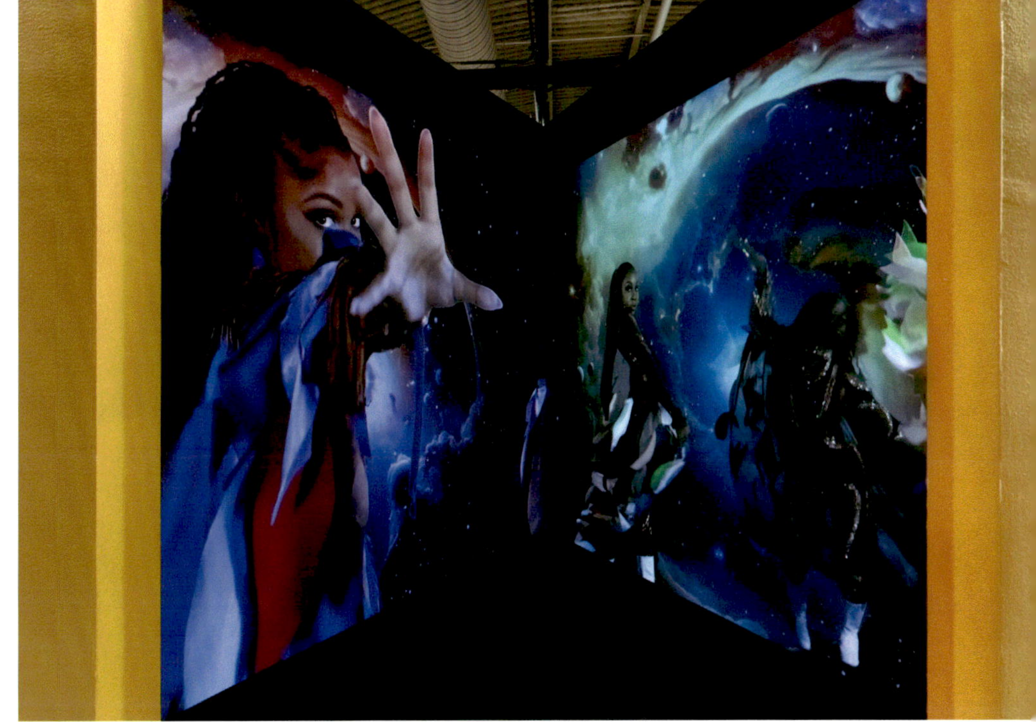

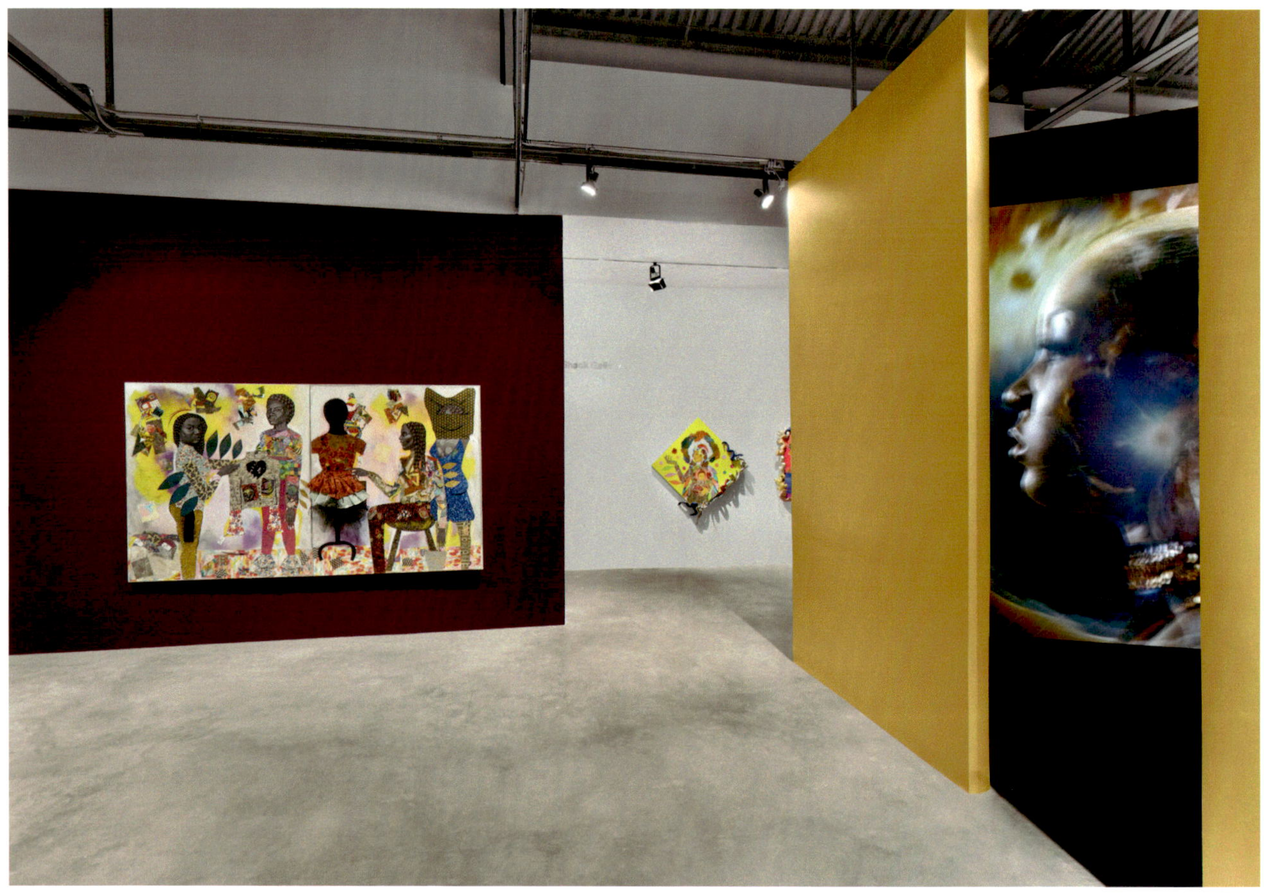

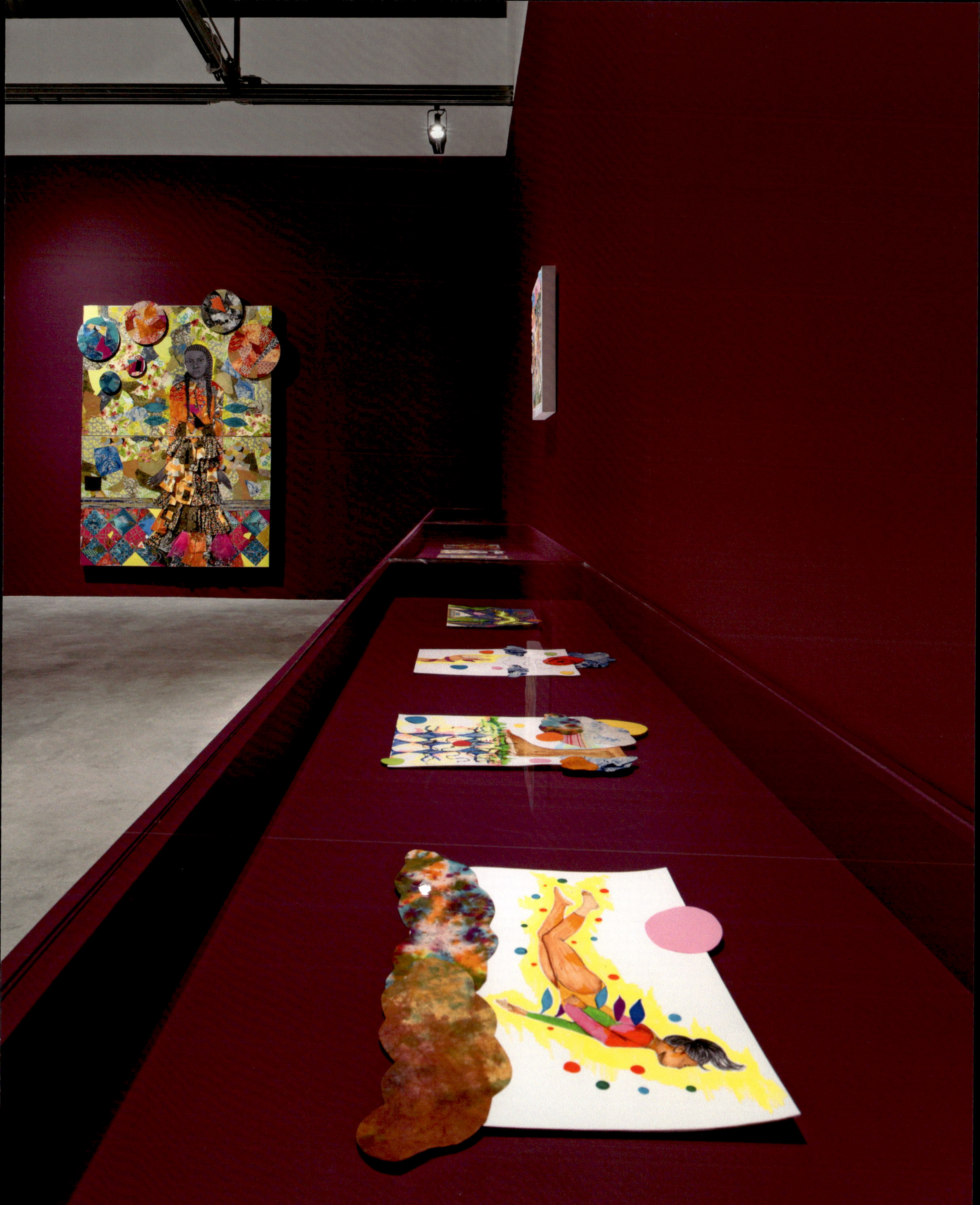

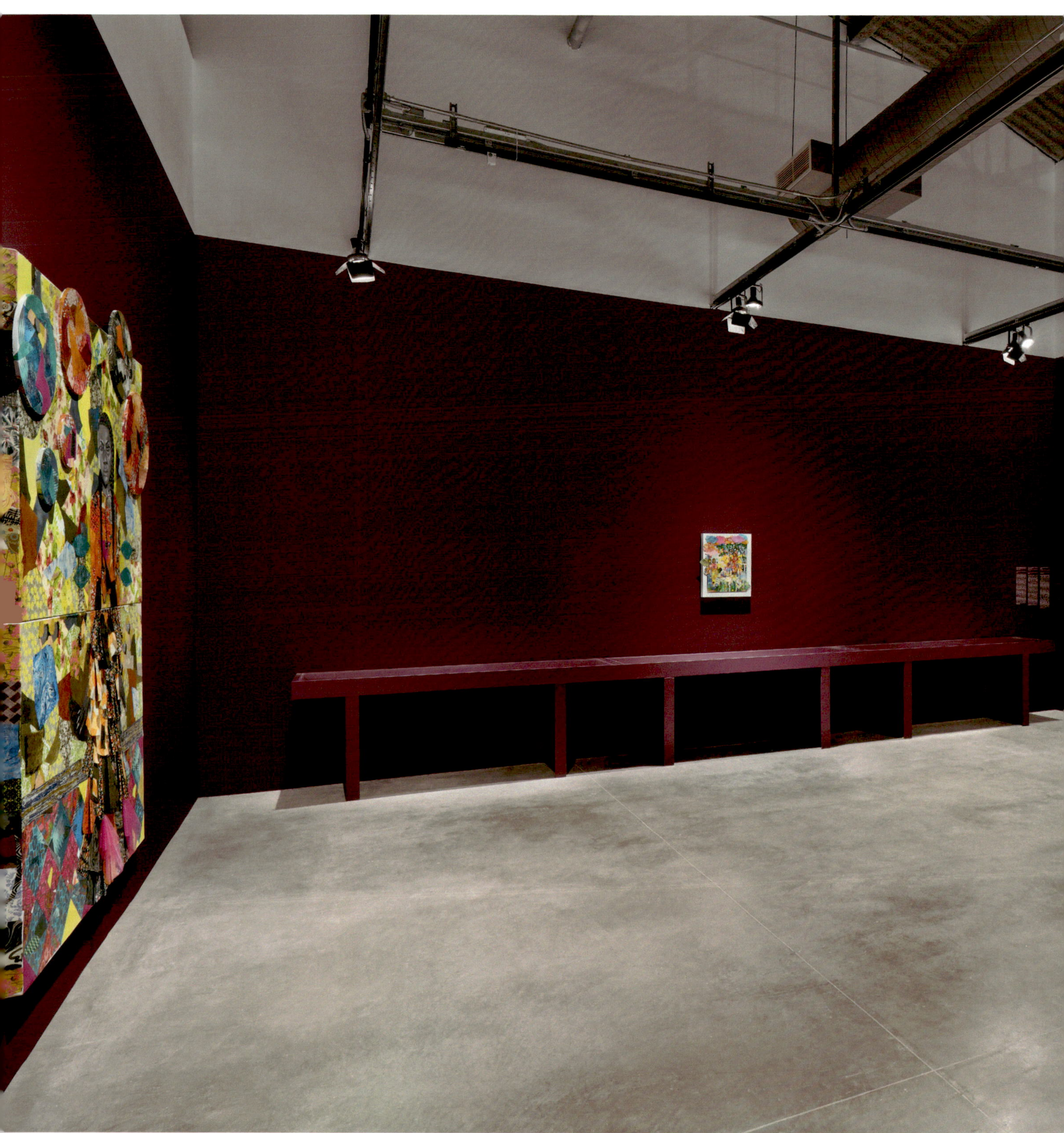

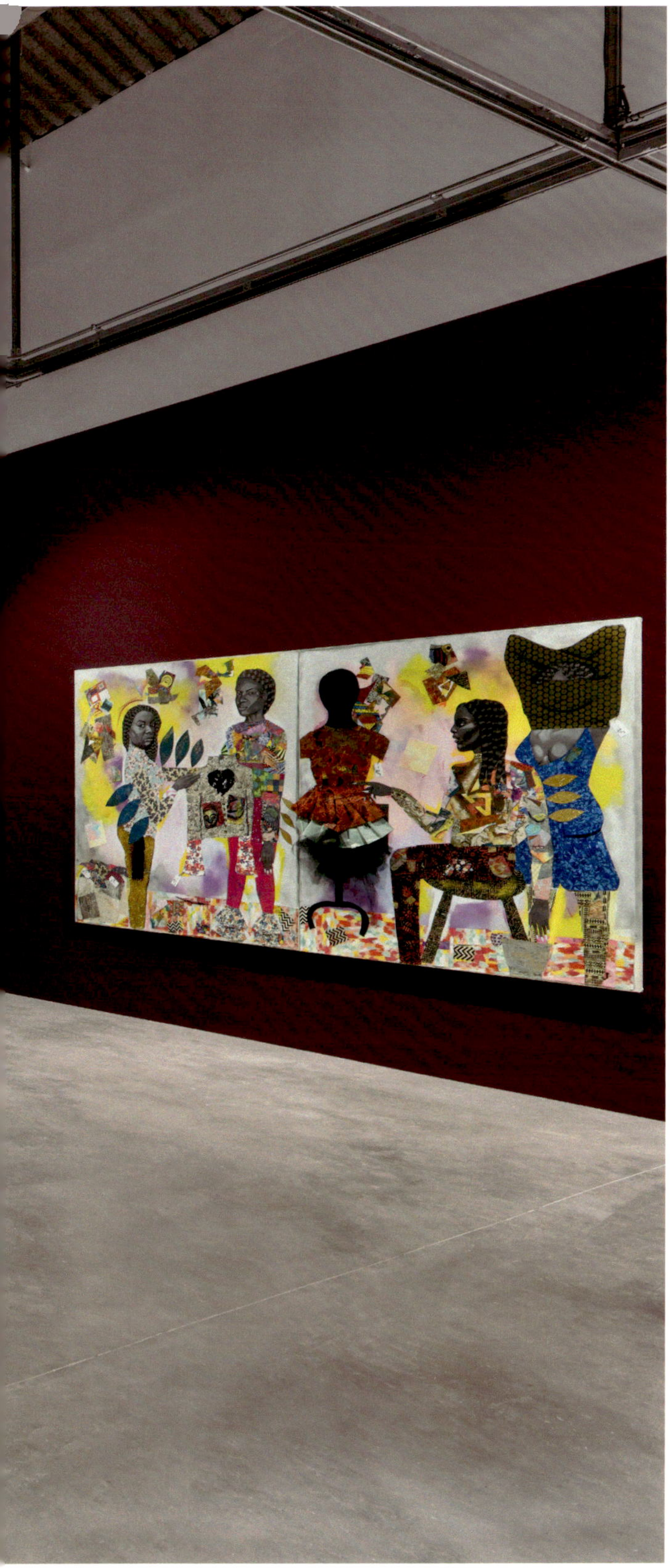

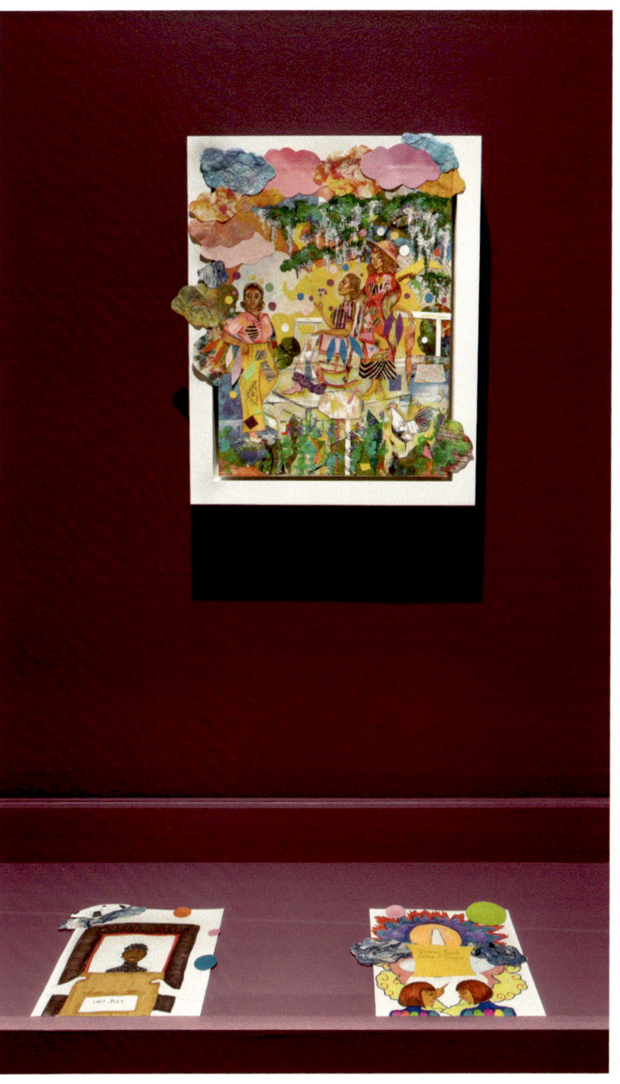

LIST OF EXHIBITED WORKS

Unless otherwise noted, exhibited works are courtesy of the artist and Kravets Wehby Gallery.

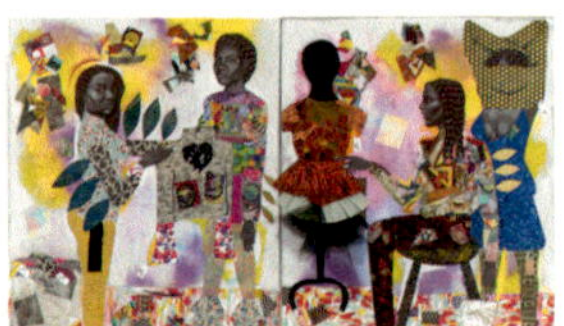

Shirt with Lace Heart (diptych), 2018
Acrylic, spray paint, glitter, ink, and collage on canvas
72 × 128 in. overall
Courtesy of Rubell Museum, Miami and Washington, DC
pp. 38–39

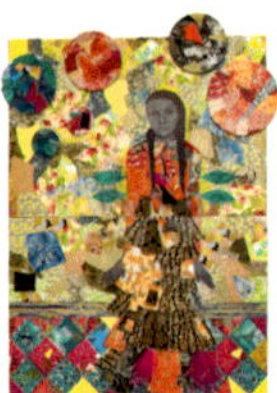

The Prettiest Dress (diptych), 2019
Ink, acrylic, mixed media, colored pencil, fabric, glitter, and rhinestones on canvas
96 × 72 in. overall
Collection of Beth Rudin DeWoody
p. 8

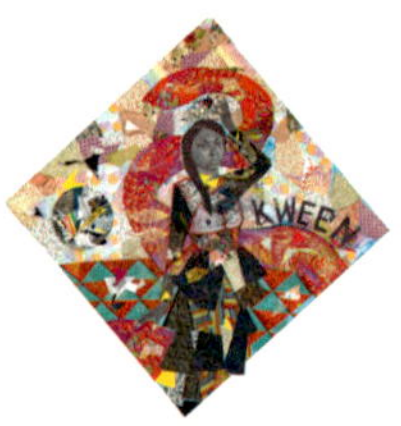

Prom Kween, 2019
Ink, acrylic, mixed media, colored pencil, fabric, glitter, and rhinestones on canvas
77 × 72 in.
Private collection
p. 37

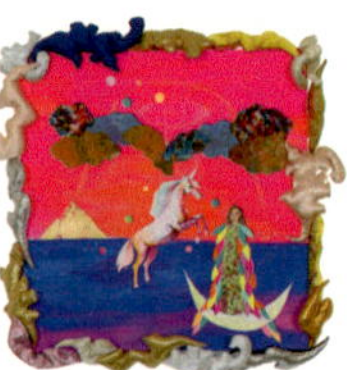

A Girl and Her Unicorn, 2023
Acrylic, gold leaf, glitter, mixed-media collage, and soft sculpture on canvas
46 × 46 in.
p. 32

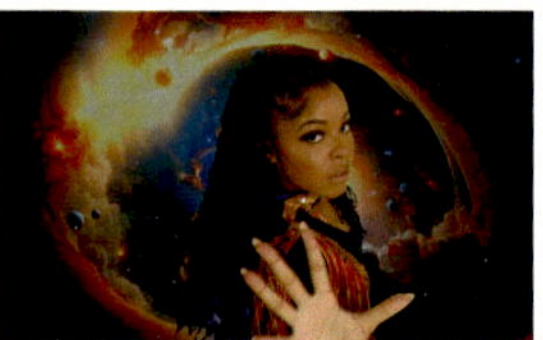

Ancient Future, 2023
Digital film, color, sound; 7 minutes
pp. 12, 48–61

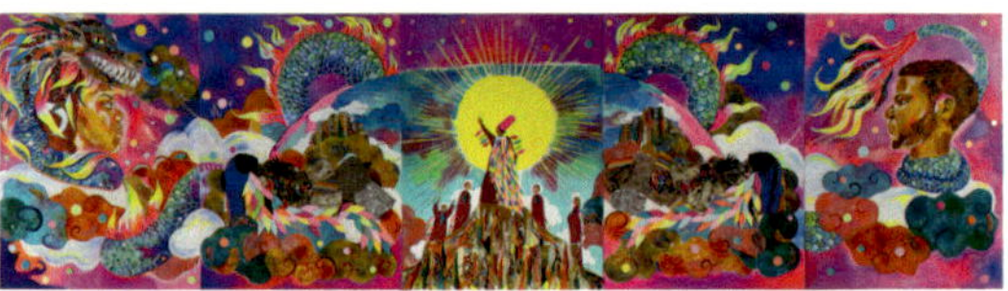

Dark Night of the Soul, 2023
Acrylic, gold leaf, glitter, mixed-media collage, and soft sculpture on canvas
96 × 360 in. overall
pp. 10–11, 34–35

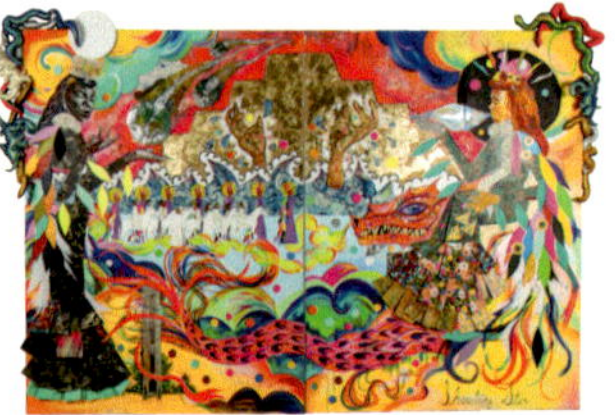

Lullaby for a Shooting Star (diptych), 2023
Acrylic, gold leaf, glitter, mixed-media collage, and soft sculpture on canvas
96 × 144 in. overall
Collection of Scott R. Coleman
Cover, p. 40

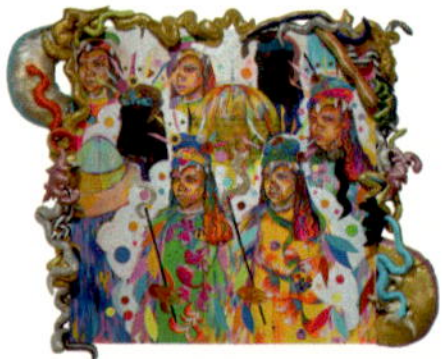

March of the Nagas, 2023
Acrylic, silver leaf, rhinestones, glitter, mixed-media collage, and soft sculpture on canvas
72 × 72 in.

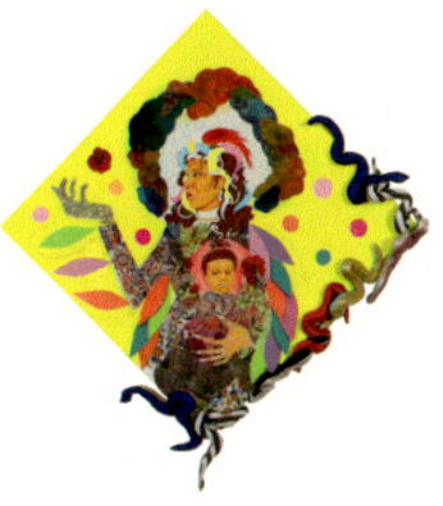

Mother and Child, 2023
Acrylic, gold leaf, glitter, mixed-media collage, and soft sculpture on canvas
46 × 46 in.
p. 31

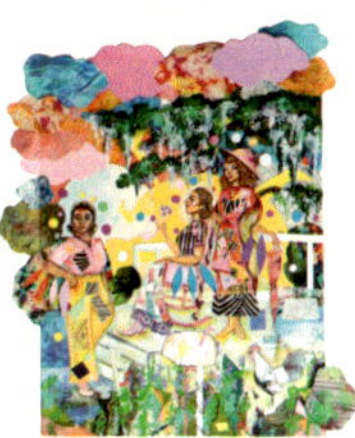

She Who Crowned Herself, 2022–23
Marker, colored pencil, and mixed-media collage on canvas
20 × 16 in.
p. 41

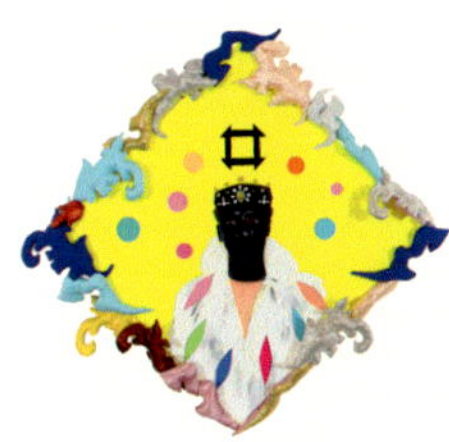

The Man, The Myth, The Legend, 2023
Acrylic, rhinestones, glitter, mixed-media collage, and soft sculpture on canvas
46 × 46 in.
p. 30

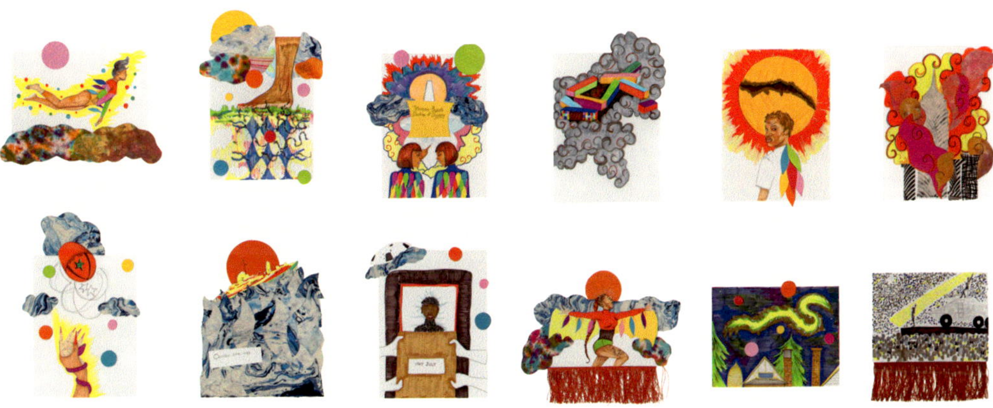

The Unraveling (suite of 12 drawings), 2023
Marker, colored pencil, and mixed-media collage on paper
9 × 12 in. each, unframed
pp. 42–45

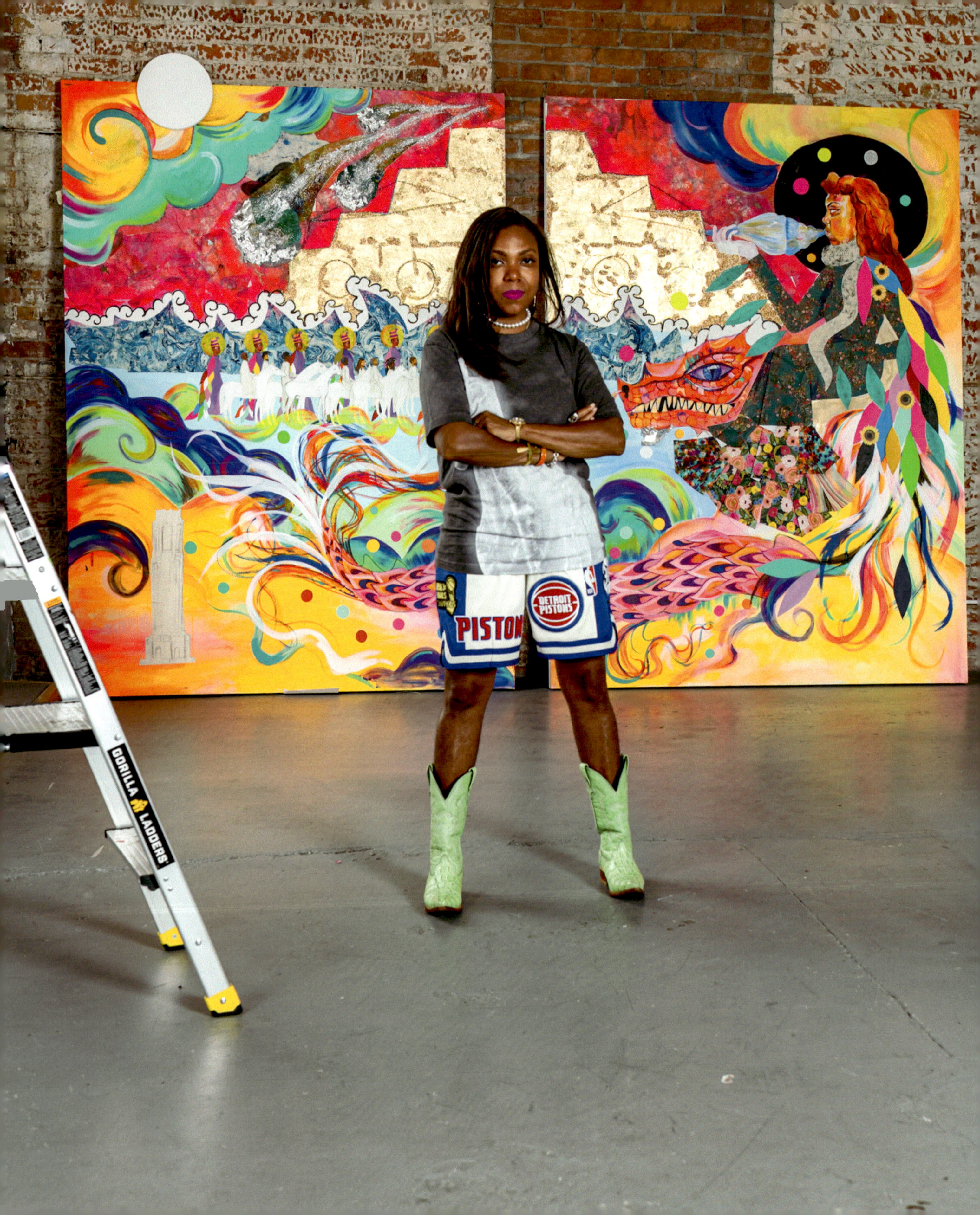

DETROIT PISTONS
PISTON
GORILLA LADDERS

Born 1982, Detroit, MI
Lives and works in Detroit, MI

Education

Howard University, Washington, DC
MFA, 2012

Jackson State University, Jackson, MS
BFA, 2004

Tougaloo Art Colony, Tougaloo, MS
Art Residency, 2003

Solo Exhibitions

2023 *Ancient Future*, Museum of Contemporary Art, North Miami, FL

2022 *Currency*, Kravets Wehby Gallery, New York, NY
Currency, Library Street Collective, Detroit, MI
We're a Wonder: Perspectives on Black Experience | Jamea Richmond-Edwards, Dr. William R. Harvey Museum of Art, Talladega, AL, and the Carr Center, Detroit, MI

2020 *Twenty Twenty*, South Bend Museum of Art, South Bend, IN

2019 *7 Mile Girls*, Rowan University Art Gallery, Glassboro, NJ
Prom Night, Kravets Wehby Gallery, New York, NY
Stay Fly, CulturalDC, Washington, DC

2018 *Fly Girl Fly*, Kravets Wehby Gallery, New York, NY

2017 *Athena Shrugged (2)*, Long-Sharp Gallery, New York, NY

2016 *Mosaic Project*, Pennsylvania College of Art and Design, Lancaster, PA
Take Me Away, Southern Gallery, Charleston, SC

2015 *The Cost of Making Her Run,* The N'Namdi Center for Contemporary Art, Detroit, MI

2014 *The Cost of Making Her Run: Fear, Flight, Freedom,* DC Arts Center, Washington, DC

2012 *Shrines*, Morton Fine Art, Washington, DC

2005 *Femininity,* Bucketworks, Milwaukee, WI

Group Exhibitions

2023 *Multiplicity: Blackness in Contemporary American Collage,* Frist Art Museum, Nashville, TN; Museum of Fine Arts, Houston, TX; The Phillips Collection, Washington, DC
PRESENT '23: Building the Scantland Collection of the Columbus Museum of Art, Columbus Museum of Art, Columbus, OH
Skilled Labor: Black Realism in Detroit, Cranbrook Art Museum, Bloomfield Hills, MI
A Movement in Every Direction: Legacies of the Great Migration, Brooklyn Museum, Brooklyn, NY; California African American Museum, Los Angeles, CA

2022 *What's Going On,* Rubell Museum, Washington, DC
Terms & Conditions, Kravets Wehby Gallery, New York, NY
A Movement in Every Direction: Legacies of the Great Migration, Mississippi Museum of Art, Jackson, MS; Baltimore Museum of Art, Baltimore, MD

2021 *Experience 49: blue/s,* ESMoA, El Segundo, CA
SITE: Michigan Central Station, Libraray Street Collective, Detroit, MI
On the Road: Chocolate Cities, TONE, Memphis, TN

2020 *Rentrée*, Kravets Wehby Gallery, New York, NY
Young Artists: One, Fridman Gallery, New York, NY
Auguries of Innocence, Fredericks & Freiser, New York, NY
CHRONICLES VOL.2, Galerie Droste, Wuppertal, Germany
Fragmented Bodies, Albertz Benda, New York, NY

2019 *Summer Fling*, Kravets Wehby Gallery, New York, NY

2018 *New Acquisitions*, Rubell Family Collection, Miami, FL
American Beauty, Kravets Wehby Gallery, New York, NY

2017 *Hi-Res*, Kravets Wehby Gallery, New York, NY
She Rocks, Kravets Wehby Gallery, New York, NY
Art of Rebellion: Black Art of the Civil Rights Movement, Charles H. Wright Museum of African American History, Detroit, MI
Building Bridges: The Politics of Love, Identity and Race, Galerie Myrtis, Baltimore, MD
Shifting: African American Women Artists and the Power of Their Gaze, David C. Driskell Center, University of Maryland, College Park, MD

2016 *Lest We Forget*, Galerie Myrtis, Baltimore, MD
It Takes a Nation: Artists for Social Justice, Katzen Arts Center, American University, Washington, DC
Circle of Friends, Katzen Arts Center, American University, Washington, DC
*History Continues: Contemporary African American Artist*s, Mosely Gallery, University of Maryland Eastern Shore, Princess Anne, MD

2015 *Topography*, Tinney Contemporary, Nashville, TN
Delusions of Grandeur: "How We Lost DC," Honfleur Gallery, Washington, DC
FLUX Art Fair, Harlem, NY

2014 Prizm Art Fair, Miami, FL
Romare Bearden, Terry Brodie, Kesha Bruce and Jamea Richmond-Edwards, Clifford Chance US LLP, New York, NY; Washington, DC
Assembled, Whitney Center for the Arts, Pittsfield, MA

2013 *SELECT 2013,* Washington, DC
Delusions of Grandeur: "No Strings Attached," 39th Street Gallery, Brentwood, MD
Revealing the African Presence in Renaissance Europe: The Contemporary Response, Galerie Myrtis, in conjunction with Walters Art Museum, Baltimore, MD

2012 *To Be Young, Gifted and Black in the Age of Obama,* Kentler International Drawing Space, Brooklyn, NY
Fashioned in Time, Corridor Gallery/Rush Philanthropic, Brooklyn, NY

2011 *Visions, Voices and Viewpoints of African American Artists,* Peltz Gallery, Milwaukee, WI
Delusions of Grandeur: "Ascension," Parish Gallery, Washington, DC
Delusions of Grandeur, Mandarin Oriental, Washington, DC

2010 *FOCUS GROUP: Four Walls, Four Women,* DC Arts Center, Washington, DC
Pretty Things, Little Treasures and Hidden Meanings, AYN Studios, Washington, DC
Modus Union, Art Whino, Washington, DC
Women of the African Diaspora: Images of Hope & Struggle, Fellowship Hall, Wesley United Methodist Church, Washington, DC

2009 *Coexist,* Broadway Theatre Center, Milwaukee, WI

2006 *The Uncommon Icon: Reinventing the Sacred,* Uihlein Peters Gallery, Milwaukee, WI

Grants

2018 Joan Mitchell Foundation Painters & Sculptors Grant

SELECTED BIBLIOGRAPHY

Armstrong, Annie. "Joan Mitchell Foundation Names Recipients of 2018 Painters & Sculptors Grants." *Art News,* December 12, 2018, https://www.artnews.com/art-news/news/joan-mitchell-foundation-announced-recipients-2018-painters-sculptors-grants-11518/.

Artists & Makers. "Telling Stories in Portraits." Winter 2015: 80.

Artsy. "Black Women Turn Inward and Take Flight in Jamea Richmond-Edwards' Powerful New Portraits." October 6, 2016, https://www.artsy.net/article/artsy-black-women-turn-inward-and-take-flight-in-jamea-richmond-edwards-powerful-new-portraits.

Carroll, Angela N. "Lest We Forget." *BmoreArt,* October 13, 2016, https://bmoreart.com/2016/10/lest-we-forget.html.

Cascone, Sarah. "Editors' Picks: 19 Things to See in New York this Week." *Artnet News*, April 23, 2018, https://news.artnet.com/art-world/editors-picks-april-23-1262492.

Charleston City Paper. "Jamea Richmond-Edwards' Art Tackles the War on Drugs." September 21, 2016, https://charlestoncitypaper.com/2016/09/21/jamea-richmond-edwards-art-tackles-the-war-on-drugs/.

Contemporary And. "Jamea Richmond-Edwards: Prom Night." October 17, 2019, https://contemporaryand.com/exhibition/jamea-richmond-edwards-prom-night/.

Cotter, Holland. "For Black Artists, the Great Migration Is an Unfinished Journey." *New York Times,* August 4, 2022, https://www.nytimes.com/2022/08/04/arts/design/black-artists-migration-mississippi-museum-art-review.html.

Delson, Susan. "Imagining the Great Migration." *Wall Street Journal,* October 14, 2022, https://www.wsj.com/articles/imagining-the-great-migration-11665770596.

Dreifus, Claudia. "A Tribute to Black Artists Could Signal a Change for Museums." *New York Times,* October 20, 2022, https://www.nytimes.com/2022/10/20/arts/design/black-artists-african-art.html.

Drinkard, Jane. "The Artist Exploring Black Women's Relationship to Luxury Clothing." *The Cut,* April 11, 2018, https://www.thecut.com/2018/04/artist-explores-politics-of-black-women-and-luxury-clothing.html.

Hodges, Michael. "Art of Transformative Rebellion at Wright Museum, DIA." *Detroit News,* July 21, 2017, https://www.detroitnews.com/story/entertainment/arts/2017/07/21/dia-wright-detroit-riot-rebellion-exhibitions/103908042/.

Huffington Post. "Black Artists: 30 Contemporary Art Makers Under 40 You Should Know." February 26, 2013, https://www.huffpost.com/entry/black-artists-under-40-contemporary-painters-sculptors-performance-race-representation-art_n_2725639.

Jenkins, Mark. "In the Galleries: 'Afrofuturism,' Defined in the Moment, by Nine Artists." *Washington Post.* September 7, 2017, https://www.washingtonpost.com/entertainment/museums/in-the-galleries-afrofuturism-defined-in-the-moment-by-nine-artists/2017/09/07/740a5428-924d-11e7-89fa-bb822a46da5b_story.html.

———. "Women's Artwork Is Never Done." *Washington Post*, February 25, 2016, https://www.washingtonpost.com/goingoutguide/museums/womens-artwork-is-never-done/2016/02/25/1e423d50-d690-11e5-b195-2e29a4e13425_story.html.

Nolan, Joe. "Black Art Matters in 'Topography,' at Tinney Contemporary, Nashville." *Burnaway,* November 19, 2015, https://burnaway.org/daily/black-art-matters-topography-tinney/.

Rodney, Seph. "A Show About the Great Migration Strikes a Timely Chord." *Hyperallergic,* June 21, 2022, https://hyperallergic.com/741854/a-show-about-the-great-migration-strikes-a-timely-chord/.

Rowell, Charles Henry. "Jamea Richmond-Edwards." *Callaloo* 38, no. 4 (2015): 847–50, 938–42.

Sanders, Marlisa. "Family Turmoil was the Creative Spark for a Young Artist." *International Review of African American Art Plus*, February 20, 2013, available at https://galeriemyrtis.net/uploads/press/Jamea_Richmond-IRAAA-2-20-2013.pdf.

Sargent, Antwaun. "An Artist Finds Her Family's Glamour in the Crack Epidemic." *Vice,* January 19, 2016, https://www.vice.com/en/article/9an838/jamea-richmond-edwards-paintings.

Sharp, Sarah Rose. "Calling Detroit's 1967 Civil Unrest a 'Rebellion,' a Museum Takes a Strong Stand." *Hyperallergic,* October 23, 2017, https://hyperallergic.com/396619/calling-detroits-1967-civil-unrest-a-rebellion-a-museum-takes-a-strong-stand/.

Sheets, Hilarie M. "New Exhibition Focusing on 'Legacies of the Great Migration' Looks at Artists' Personal Connections to a Chapter of U.S. History." *Art News,* April 4, 2022, https://www.artnews.com/art-news/news/legacies-of-the-great-migration-exhibition-preview-1234623533/#!.

Sherman, John. "How the Identity Politics of 'Empire' Play Out on Its Walls." *Hyperallergic,* April 27, 2015, https://hyperallergic.com/202183/how-the-identity-politics-of-empire-play-out-on-its-walls/.

Valentine, Victoria L. "Artist Jamea Richmond-Edwards Explores Issues of Identity, Perception, and the Lure of Luxe Goods." *Culture Type,* April 20, 2018, https://www.culturetype.com/2018/04/20/artist-jamea-richmond-edwards-explores-issues-of-identity-perception-and-the-lure-of-luxe-goods/.

Vora, Vinesh. "Harlem Introduces Its First Ever Contemporary Art Fair." *The Source,* May 16, 2015, https://thesource.com/2015/05/16/harlem-introduces-its-first-ever-contemporary-art-fair/.

Yancheva, Natalia. "The Must-See Exhibition in New York This Month." *L'Officiel,* April 12, 2018, https://www.lofficielusa.com/art/must-see-exhibition-in-new-york-this-weekend.

CONTRIBUTOR BIOGRAPHIES

TAYLOR RENEE ALDRIDGE is a curator and writer from Detroit, Michigan. She joined the California African American Museum (CAAM) in August 2020. Aldridge has organized critically acclaimed exhibitions with the Detroit Institute of Arts, Detroit Artists Market, Cranbrook Art Museum, and The Luminary (St. Louis). In 2015, along with art critic Jessica Lynne, she cofounded *ARTS.BLACK*, an influential journal of art criticism for Black perspectives. Her writing has appeared in *Artforum*, *The Art Newspaper*, *Art21*, *Art News*, *Canadian Art*, *Contemporary And*, *Detroit Metro Times*, *Hyperallergic*, and SFMOMA's *Open Space*. She was the recipient of the 2016 Creative Capital | Andy Warhol Foundation Arts Writers Grant for Short Form Writing and the 2019 Rabkin Foundation Award for Art Journalism. She holds an MLA from Harvard University with a concentration in museum studies and a BA from Howard University with a concentration in art history.

NIAMA SAFIA SANDY is a New York–based cultural anthropologist, curator, producer, organizer, multidisciplinary artist, and musician. Her creative practice delves into the human story through the application and critical lenses of culture, healing, history, migration, music, race, and ritual. Sandy's aim is to leverage history and the visual, written, and performative arts—chiefly those of the Global Black Diaspora—to tell stories we know in ways we have not yet thought to tell them and to lift us all to a higher state of historical, ontological, and spiritual wholeness in the process. She has participated in and convened programs at TEDWomen, Schomburg Center for Research in Black Culture, MICA, Harvard University, Oberlin College, the Public Theater, and the Brooklyn Museum. Sandy and her work have been featured in *Artsy*, *The New York Times*, *Monopol*, *Teen Vogue*, *The Washington Post*, *Hyperallergic*, *Camera Austria*, and *OkayAfrica*. She is a founding curator of the Southeast Queens Biennial, cofounder of the Blacksmiths and THIS IS A MOVEMENT, and an active member of the artist collectives Resistance Revival Chorus and Wide Awakes. She is currently a visiting assistant professor at Pratt Institute's School of Art.

ADEZE WILFORD is a curator at the Museum of Contemporary Art, North Miami, where she has organized *Leah Gordon: Kanaval* (2022) and *Lonnie Holley: If You Really Knew* and *The South Florida Cultural Consortium* (2023). She was an assistant curator at The Shed, where she organized *Howardena Pindell: Rope/Fire/Water,* and an inaugural joint curatorial fellow at the Studio Museum in Harlem and the Museum of Modern Art, New York. She organized *Vernacular Interior* (2019) at Hales Gallery, *Excerpt* (2017) at the Studio Museum, and a film series, *Black Intimacy* (2017), at MoMA. Other curatorial projects include *Harlem Postcards* (2016–17) and *Color in Shadows*, the 2016 Expanding the Walls exhibition at the Studio Museum. Prior to this, Wilford was the public programs and community engagement assistant at the Studio Museum. She has contributed scholarship to various catalogues and magazines, including *Young, Gifted and Black*, *Black Refractions*, and *Art in America*, and serves on the Queens Museum Board. She graduated from Northwestern University with a BA in art history and African American studies.

ACKNOWLEDGMENTS

Jamea Richmond-Edwards: Ancient Future was made possible with major support from the Andy Warhol Foundation for the Visual Arts and Kravets Wehby Gallery. Additional support was provided by MOCA Visionaries.

MOCA North Miami is generously funded by the North Miami Mayor and Council and the City of North Miami; the John S. and James L. Knight Foundation; and the Miami-Dade County Department of Cultural Affairs and the Cultural Affairs Council, the Miami-Dade County Mayor and Board of County Commissioners. MOCA is sponsored in part by the State of Florida through the Division of Arts and Culture and the National Endowment for the Arts. Additional support is provided by the Fine & Greenwald Foundation and the Sol Taplin Charitable Foundation. Founding support for the MOCA Sustainability Fund was provided by the Green Family Foundation Trust. We also thank our Board of Trustees, Curator's Circle, and MOCA Members for their meaningful support.

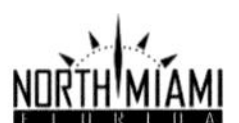

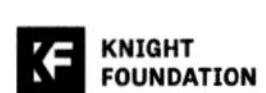

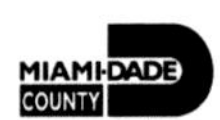

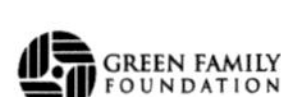

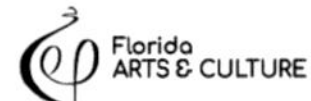

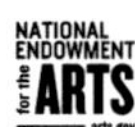

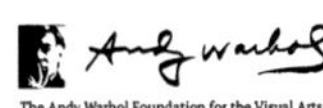

KRAVETS|WEHBY

BOARD OF TRUSTEES

CITY OF NORTH MIAMI

Alix Deslume, EdD	*Mayor*
Mary Estimé-Irvin	*Vice Mayor, District 3*
Scott Galvin	*District 1 Councilman*
Kassandra Timothe, MPA	*District 2 Councilwoman*
Pierre Frantz Charles, EdM	*District 4 Councilman*
Rasha Cameau, MBA, FRA-RP	*North Miami City Manager*

STAFF LIST

Chana Budgazad Sheldon	*Executive Director*
T. J. Black	*Deputy Director*
Akilah Child	*Director of Communications*
Amanda Covach	*Curator of Education*
Sara Ryan	*Director of Development*
Adeze Wilford	*Curator*
Lauren Baccus	*Public Program Manager*
Lorraine Biaggi	*Membership + Donor Relations Manager*
Sophie Bonet	*Exhibitions Manager*
Arasay Vazquez Diaz	*Registrar*
Lucero Gronquist	*Finance Manager*
Kimari Jackson	*Curatorial Assistant*
Shekinah Johnson	*Development Assistant*
Marceau Livette	*Chief of Security*
Francesca Mancuso	*Youth Education Manager*
Gina Martins	*Event + Program Coordinator*
Eric Mendoza	*Graphic Designer*
Fabienne Merritt	*Content Manager + Copywriter*
William Miranda	*Building Manager*
Maria Pereira	*Executive Assistant*
Felix St. Hilaire	*Gallery Interpreter*
Tainisel Rodriguez	*Guest Experience Manager*

Editor
Adeze Wilford

Managing Editor + Production
Todd Bradway

Design
Dian Holton

Jamea Richmond-Edwards: Ancient Future is published in conjunction with the exhibition curated by Adeze Wilford and presented at the Museum of Contemporary Art, North Miami, October 25, 2023–March 17, 2024

Published by

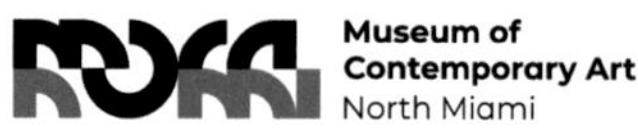

Museum of Contemporary Art, North Miami
770 NE 125th Street
North Miami, FL 33161
Mocanomi.org

Printed and bound by GHP, West Haven, CT

Printed on McCoy Silk 100 lb.
Typeset in Copperplate, Raleway, and Times

ISBN
979-8-9871852-2-3

Library of Congress Control Number
2023915401

Distributed by
ARTBOOK | D.A.P.
75 Broad Street, Suite 630
New York, NY 10004
Artbook.com

Printed in the United States of America

Cover: *Lullaby for a Shooting Star* (diptych), 2023. Detail
pp. 2–3, 80: Jamea Richmond-Edwards in her Detroit studio, 2023
pp. 64–77: *Jamea Richmond-Edwards: Ancient Future*, Museum of Contemporary Art, North Miami, 2023–24. Installation views

Photo Credits
Zachary Balber: cover, pp. 8, 10–12, 22, 30–35, 37–43, 64-77
Cortney Leatherwood: pp. 2–3, 80

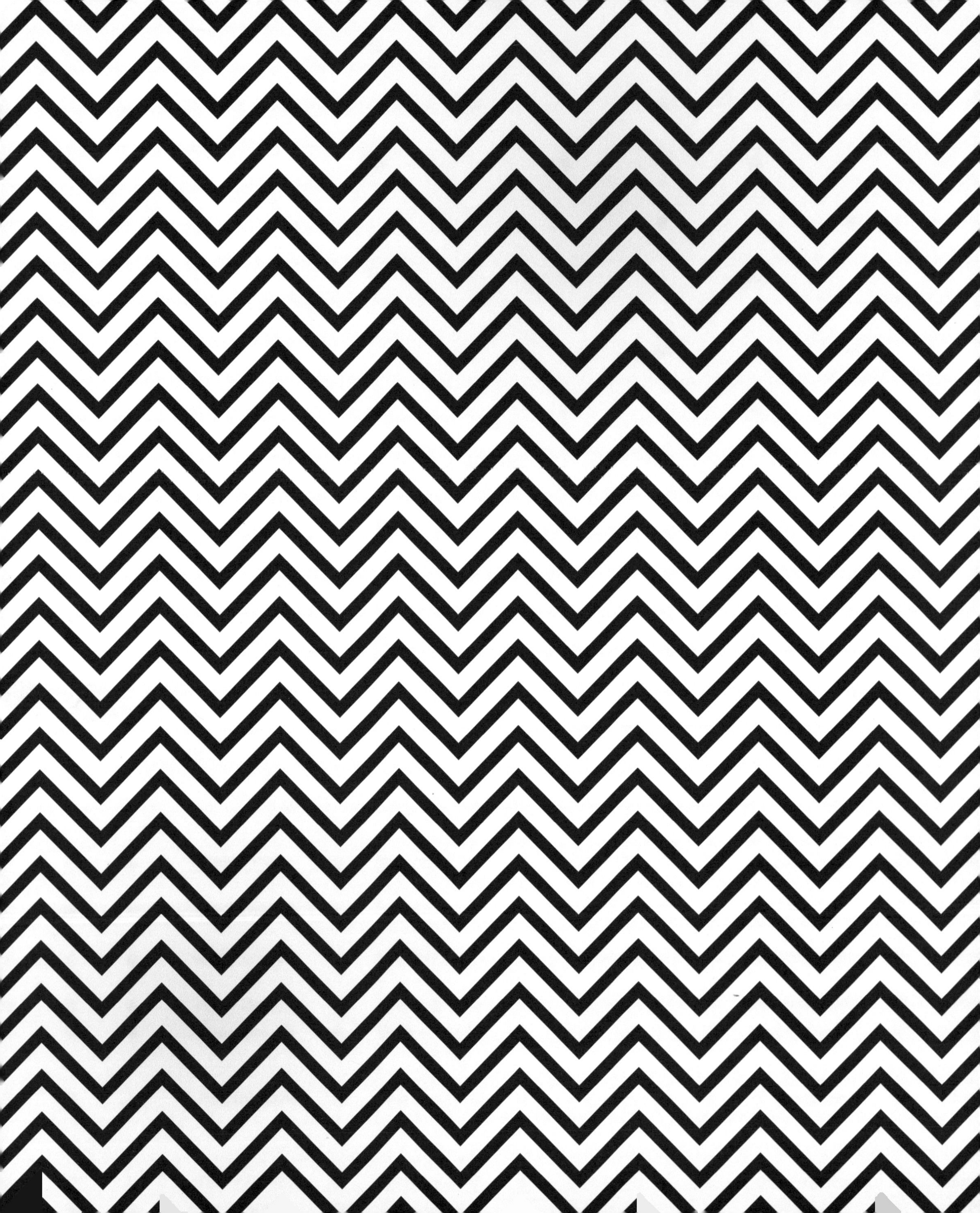